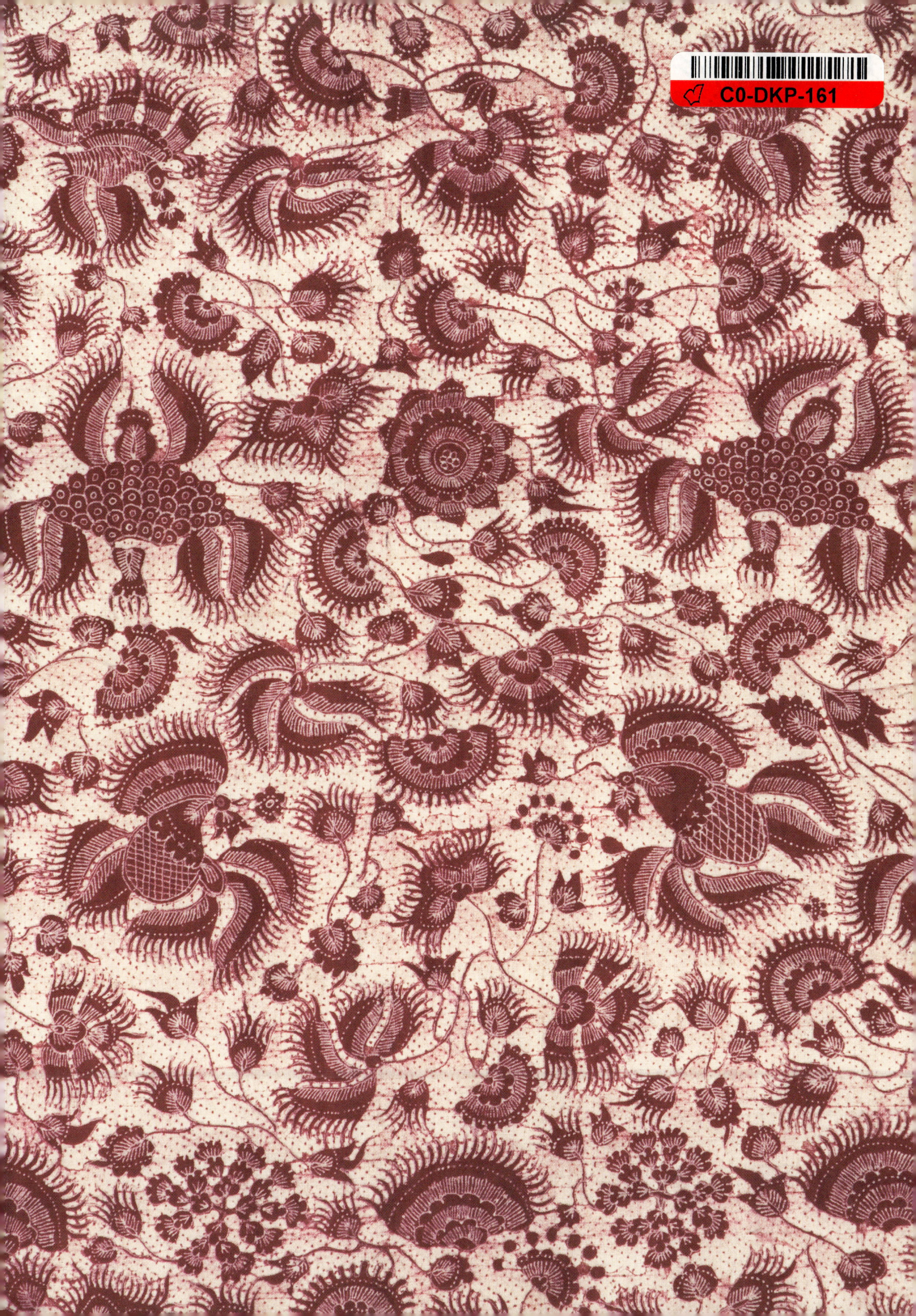

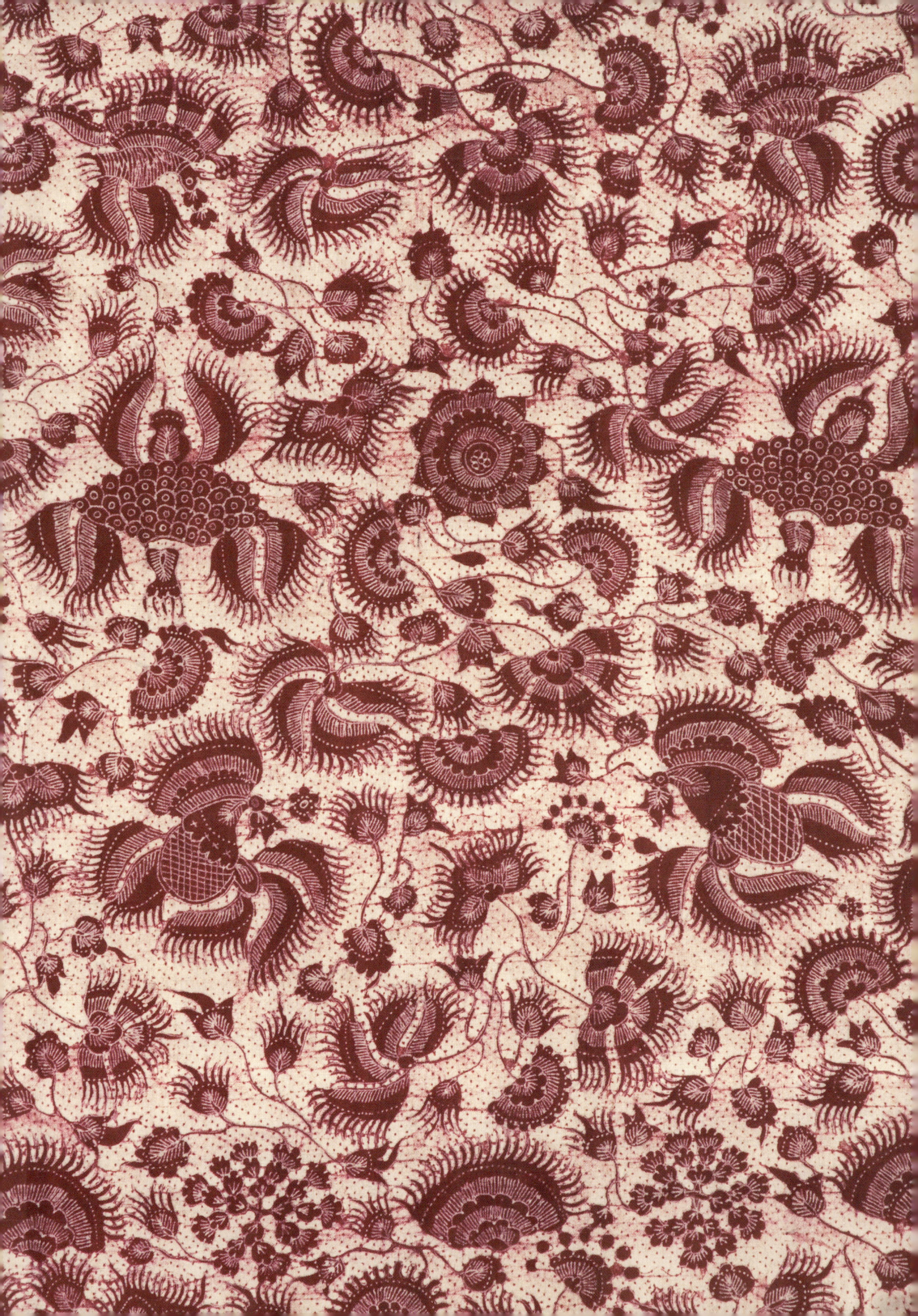

NINI TOWOK'S SPINNING WHEEL

Nini Towok's Spinning Wheel

....

CLOTH AND THE CYCLE OF LIFE IN KEREK, JAVA

Rens Heringa

FOWLER MUSEUM AT UCLA
LOS ANGELES

Fowler Museum Textile Series, No. 9

Textile Series Editorial Board
Marla C. Berns
Patricia Rieff Anawalt
Roy W. Hamilton
Betsy D. Quick
Lynne Kostman
Danny Brauer

FOWLER MUSEUM
Textile Series

Funding for this publication and the accompanying exhibition was provided by

R. L. Shep Endowment
Fowler Museum Textile Council
Cotsen Foundation for Academic Research

The Fowler Museum is part of UCLA's School of the Arts and Architecture

Lynne Kostman, *Managing Editor*
Danny Brauer, *Designer and Production Manager*
Don Cole, *Principal Photographer*
David Fuller, *Cartographer*

©2010 Regents of the University of California.
All rights reserved.

Fowler Museum at UCLA
Box 951549
Los Angeles, California 90095-1549

Requests for permission to reproduce material from this volume should be sent to the Fowler Museum Publications Department at the above address.

Printed and bound in Hong Kong by Great Wall Printing Company Limited.

Library of Congress Cataloging-in-Publication Data

Heringa, Rens.
  Nini Towok's spinning wheel : cloth and the cycle of life in Kerek, Java / Rens Heringa.
     p. cm. — (Fowler Museum textile series ; no. 9)
  ISBN 978-0-9778344-2-6 (pbk.)
  1. Textile fabrics—Indonesia—Kerek. 2. Hand weaving—Indonesia—Kerek. 3. Clothing and dress—Social aspects—Indonesia—Kerek. 4. Kerek (Indonesia)—Social life and customs. I. Fowler Museum at UCLA. II. Title. III. Title: Cloth and the cycle of life in Kerek, Java.
  NK9503.2.I52J3845 2010
  746.40959828—dc22

                                          2010008401

Front end sheet, see cat. no. 28; p. 4, see cat. no. 35; p. 5, see cat. no. 39; p. 6, see cat. no. 52; p. 9, see cat. no. 21; back end sheet, see cat. no. 54.

Contents

FOREWORD 7

PREFACE 8

INTRODUCTION 10

SPECIALIZATION IN THE HAMLETS OF KEREK 12

DRESS IN KEREK 14

THE DESIGN FORMATS OF KEREK CLOTHS 18

LAND OWNERSHIP, SOCIAL CLASS,
AND TEXTILE TECHNIQUES IN KEREK 20

THE PATTERNING OF BATIK CLOTH:
FLORAL OR ABSTRACT 30

COLOR IN KEREK BATIKS 34

NINI TOWOK'S SPINNING WHEEL 40

NINI TOWOK, THE CARDINAL DIRECTIONS,
AND THE CYCLES OF COLOR AND LIFE 42

THE DRESS OF INDIVIDUALS 44

RECENT CHANGES IN KEREK 80

BATIK IN THE TUBAN REGION 84

GLOSSARY OF FREQUENTLY USED TERMS 90

ABOUT THE AUTHOR 92

Foreword

This project marks the Fowler Museum's sixth major foray into the world of Southeast Asian textiles since 1994. Previous efforts have focused on the island of Flores in Indonesia, the Iban people of Borneo, the southern Philippines, the Minangkabau of Sumatra, and, most recently, bast and leaf fiber textiles from across the region. This time we turn to a single community, the district of Kerek in rural East Java. Today, despite its small size and out-of-the-way location, this community justifiably looms large in the annals of Indonesian textile history. That it does so is entirely due to the lifelong efforts of the author of this volume, Rens Heringa, who recognized the importance of Kerek's textile traditions, documented them, and brought them to the attention of the outside world. This publication represents her most comprehensive treatment of the subject to date. The Fowler Museum's senior curator for Asian and Pacific collections, Roy W. Hamilton, worked extensively with Rens in planning and developing this book and the exhibition that accompanies it.

The Fowler Museum's ability to publish this seminal study—the ninth title in our Textile Series—is due in large part to the generosity of Robb Shep, who has established an endowment at UCLA to support the Museum's textile publications and textile-related projects. A second exhibition and publication, *Weaver's Stories from Island Southeast Asia* by Hamilton, will coincide with *Nini Towok*, and more are planned for the near future. We sincerely hope that our efforts will justify the faith Robb Shep has placed in our institution, as well as whet his lifelong appetite for fascinating and sometimes little-known textile subjects.

Additional support for the exhibition and publication was provided by the Cotsen Foundation for Academic Research, and we thank Mary Hunt Kahlenberg for her efforts in securing this funding. Approximately half of the cloths featured in this book form part of the permanent collections of the Fowler Museum. Most of these were purchased by the Fowler Museum Textile Council, which recognized the significance of preserving this important body of previously unsung material. It was in fact the first major purchase made by this enthusiastic support group, chaired by Michael Rohde, and we thank its members for their efforts on the Museum's behalf. Additional pieces were donated to the Fowler by Mary Jane Leland, a long-time supporter of the Museum and textile specialist, and by E. M. Bakwin. They both deserve our sincerest gratitude.

As with all of our projects, every member of the Museum staff has had a role to play in a complex symphony of many and varied tasks. Their names are listed on the back page. The beauty of the book you hold in your hands is due most of all to the efforts of our publications staff—designer Danny Brauer, editor Lynne Kostman, and photographer Don Cole.

Marla C. Berns
SHIRLEY AND RALPH SHAPIRO DIRECTOR

Preface

Nearly all of the batik beloved by curators and collectors around the world comes either from the courtly environments of Central Java's interior principalities at Yogyakarta and Surakarta (also known as Solo) or from urban workshops that sprang up in the trading ports scattered along the Java Sea coast. As a result, many studies begin with a basic typological division of batik between "Central Javanese" and "North Coast" style areas. The batik in this book, however, comes from a very different source, a village setting in rural East Java. Kerek is the last place in Java where batik continues to be made on locally handwoven cotton cloth rather than on industrially produced commercial yardage. Moreover, the production and use of batik in Kerek is part of a highly integrated system of behavior and knowledge that encompasses textiles with other forms of patterning as well (including ikat and supplementary-weft weaving). Because such systems were once widespread in Java, an understanding of Kerek's textile traditions is fundamental to the textile history of the island.

Documenting and deciphering the interrelated methods and meanings of Kerek's textiles has been the career of a lifetime for Dutch textile scholar Rens Heringa. Raised in rural eastern Holland near the German border, she met her husband when they were both university students in Amsterdam. He was an Indonesian training to be a medical doctor. At the time they married in 1954, the memory of the five years of conflict between The Netherlands and Indonesia in the aftermath of the Indonesian declaration of independence in 1945 was still raw. Heringa was required under Dutch law to give up her Dutch citizenship, and she became officially stateless. In 1959, with two young children, the couple settled in Surabaya, Indonesia's second-largest city. It took determination and adaptability to raise her Indonesian-Dutch family, which grew to five children, at a time of economic and political upheaval when few mixed families, even those with generations of history in Java, chose to remain in Indonesia.

In 1976, while teaching batik to a group of expatriate wives in Surabaya, Heringa took her students with her on what was her first visit to Kerek. There she found a community, secluded in the infertile limestone hills one hundred miles west of Surabaya, that was regarded by urban Indonesians as "backward" (*kurang maju*) in the extreme. With a history of hostility toward outsiders that had made both Dutch and Indonesian authorities leery, Kerek in the early Suharto period was as yet hardly touched by the economic development that would soon bring major change. There was no electricity or piped water and little transport on the single potholed road linking Kerek to the nearest town and regional center, Tuban. Kerek's textiles were made only for local use, and few people outside the community had ever heard of them. Their rustic qualities made them the antithesis of the ideal refined (*halus*) quality prized by aficionados of Javanese batik. Heringa alone recognized the importance of what she had found, and her ability to communicate with the people of Kerek in the Javanese language allowed her to begin to understand its full significance. She continued to visit Kerek off and on even after she and her husband moved their family to Jakarta in 1979.

When her youngest child turned eighteen, Heringa went to Holland and began planning to resume the university studies she had laid aside when she married, this time with a focus on anthropology and textile studies. In 1985 she moved permanently to Leiden, where she studied under Professors Adrian Gerbrands, P. E. de Josselin de Jong, and Reimar Schefold, with Danielle Geirnaert and Sandra Niessen, who also became notable textile scholars, as her contemporaries. Heringa found it wasn't difficult to reinstate her Dutch citizenship, and she received a grant to support a period of prolonged fieldwork in Kerek in 1989–1990.

In the years since, Heringa has published extensively (see p. 92), and Kerek's importance to Indonesian textile history has come to be widely appreciated. Rather than being seen as a poor "country-cousin" or pale reflection of the better-known courtly and urban forms of batik, Kerek's textiles are now regarded as a window for understanding the full significance of textiles in Indonesian society, a last holdout that preserves forms and meanings that were once widespread but have now vanished elsewhere. Kerek itself has seen tremendous change in the last two decades (see pp. 80–83) becoming more fully integrated into Indonesia's contemporary political and economic life. A massive cement factory is now the most prominent feature of the landscape.

The rich interplay of meanings that tie together seemingly disparate cultural elements in Kerek—textile technology, mythology, color symbolism, the cardinal directions, the stages of the cycle of life—seem tailor-made for structural analysis, and that is exactly the academic tradition in which Heringa found herself immersed in Leiden. Arranging this complex web of interrelated material for an exhibition and book presented quite a challenge, but Heringa was determined to attempt something more than a straightforward piece-by-piece description of the cloths. It was her vision to arrange the textiles as "outfits" for individuals and order them according to the cardinal directions. Like all structural analyses, this requires a level of extrapolation on the part of the scholar and the audience alike, but Heringa is quick to point out that the people of Kerek themselves constantly engage in the play of categorical contrasts—light vs. dark, center vs. periphery, young vs. old, fertile vs. post-menopausal—that underlie her approach.

Ultimately we felt that the story of Nini Towok provided the best linchpin for the entire project. From her abode in the heavens, this "Granny Sunken Eyes" sends her spun cotton yarn to Earth in the form of moonbeams, providing the raw material that is the basis of Kerek's textile system and its multiple meanings. There is a double entendre here, for Nini Towok's "spinning wheel" is not just a weaver's tool; it is a metaphor for the turning of the cycle of life, and Nini herself is the one who can be seen setting it in motion on the surface of the moon in the darkened sky over Java.

Roy W. Hamilton
SENIOR CURATOR FOR ASIAN AND PACIFIC COLLECTIONS

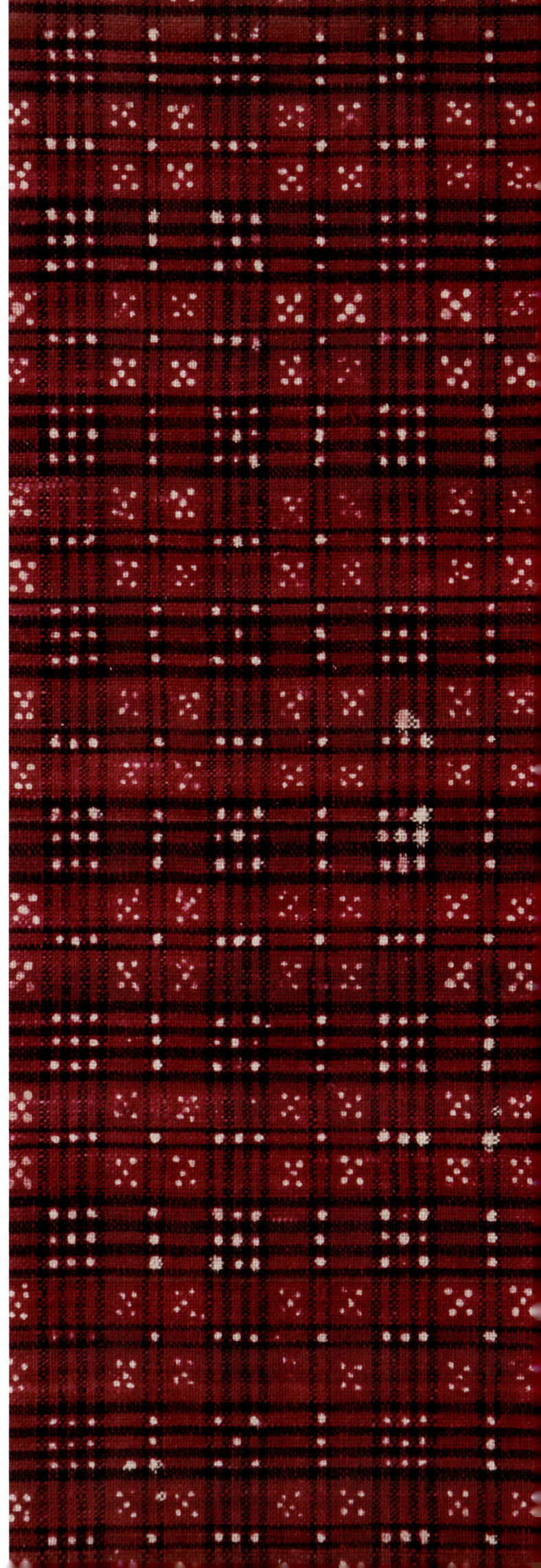

Introduction

Prior to 1830 cotton was widely grown in Java, and women were skilled at spinning it into yarn and making handwoven cloth, which was primarily used by the extended family of each weaver. A small quantity of the finest cloth was left plain and intended as the base for batik (wax-resist dyed) textiles, but more often, patterns were woven into the cloth on the loom through the use of different colors of cotton yarn.

Over the course of the nineteenth century, however, the Dutch flooded Java with increasing quantities of industrially woven white cotton cloth produced in special widths in Holland especially for use as the base cloth for batik. As a result, batik production became more and more commercialized, while Javanese handweaving went into decline. Today, only the area of Kerek continues to produce a full range of textiles with woven patterning. It also produces the only batik still made on handwoven cotton cloth.

A rural district located in the Indonesian province of East Java, Kerek is situated well off the main highways and is often regarded as culturally conservative when judged by modern urban Javanese standards. Each type of cloth made for use in Kerek is created for a specific purpose—to be worn by a person of a particular age, social, or residential group; to serve in life-cycle events such as marriages or funerals; to act as a focal point in agricultural ceremonies or curing rites. The functions, techniques, patterning, and especially the color combinations of the cloth all form part of a highly structured and elaborate system of knowledge that is remarkably integrated with the community's social organization, mythology, and ritual practices.

Remnants of similarly integrated systems of belief are known from many parts of Java, but by the late twentieth century the full system could be observed only in Kerek. Although Kerek batik is often mistakenly viewed as a poor derivative of the more-refined batiks produced in the courts of Central Java or the urban workshops of Java's North Coast, this is historically inaccurate. Rather, Kerek batik today probably represents the most direct descendant of the earliest North Coast styles, which were antecedents of both courtly and urban batik.

These banners are fashioned from two panels of heirloom cloth that would ordinarily be used to make a man's tube skirt (*sarung amba*). The blue and white color combination is regarded as protective, and the banners are paraded counterclockwise around the community when an epidemic or other calamity threatens. The pattern represents four ceremonial clubs (*bajra*) that point in the four cardinal directions to ward off evil. The name *bajra* comes from the Sanskrit *vajra*, meaning "thunderbolt," the ceremonial weapon that is a Hindu-Buddhist symbol of spiritual power.

CAT. NO. 1A,B
Pair of banners

Kerek, East Java, Indonesia, heirloom when collected in 1977. Batik on handspun/handwoven cotton cloth. Color combination: *putihan*. Pattern name: Panji serong (an honorific title, "The Honorable Oblique"). Length 225 cm. PRIVATE COLLECTION.

In every cottage there is a spinning-wheel and loom…. The operations of spinning and weaving are confined exclusively to the women, who from the highest to the lowest ranks prepare the cloths…of their families. Coloured cottons are distinguished into *luri'*…, those in which the yarn is dyed previously to weaving, and *batik*, those which are dyed subsequently.

SIR THOMAS STAMFORD RAFFLES

(1781–1826), Lieutenant-Governor of Java, 1811–1815. In *History of Java*. London: Black, Parbury, and Allen, [1817] 1978, p. 168.

Specialization in the Hamlets of Kerek

The entire population of Kerek resides in seventeen hamlets spread over an area extending roughly a three-hour walk from east to west. The hamlets are grouped in clusters according to the cardinal directions (eastern hamlets, southern hamlets, etc.) and surround the central hamlets, which occupy a middle position. The relationships among hamlet clusters are metaphorically linked to the life-cycle stages of a woman, beginning in the east (birth and childhood) and continuing through the south (sexual maturity) and west (motherhood) to the north (grandmotherhood and the end of life). The central hamlets, the "eldest" of all, have the highest status and comprise the locus of leadership and authority within Kerek.

Each of the hamlet clusters is associated with certain occupational specializations, and these form the bases for trading or exchanging textile products within the community. These relationships are also characterized according to the life-cycle stages. Thus the most "junior" process, the cultivation of cotton, is the specialization of the eastern hamlets, where there is ample land for this purpose. Middle-aged women in the western hamlets specialize in making cloth with woven patterns. Grandmothers in the northern hamlets are the most renowned spinners and weavers of the fine plain cloth used for batik. Women in all of the hamlet clusters are capable of waxing batik designs particular to their own hamlets, but high-quality batik for ceremonial use can be ordered from women residing in the central hamlets. These women—who are able to spend the long hours needed for making fine batik because they are free from the demands of agricultural labor—have to be familiar with the distinct patterns that are associated with each hamlet cluster so that they can fulfill orders. Kerek's one remaining hereditary family of dyers also resides in one of the central hamlets, and women from all areas bring their waxed cloth to this family's compound for dyeing.

FIGURE 1
The island of Java with the region of Kerek (see fig. 2) indicated.

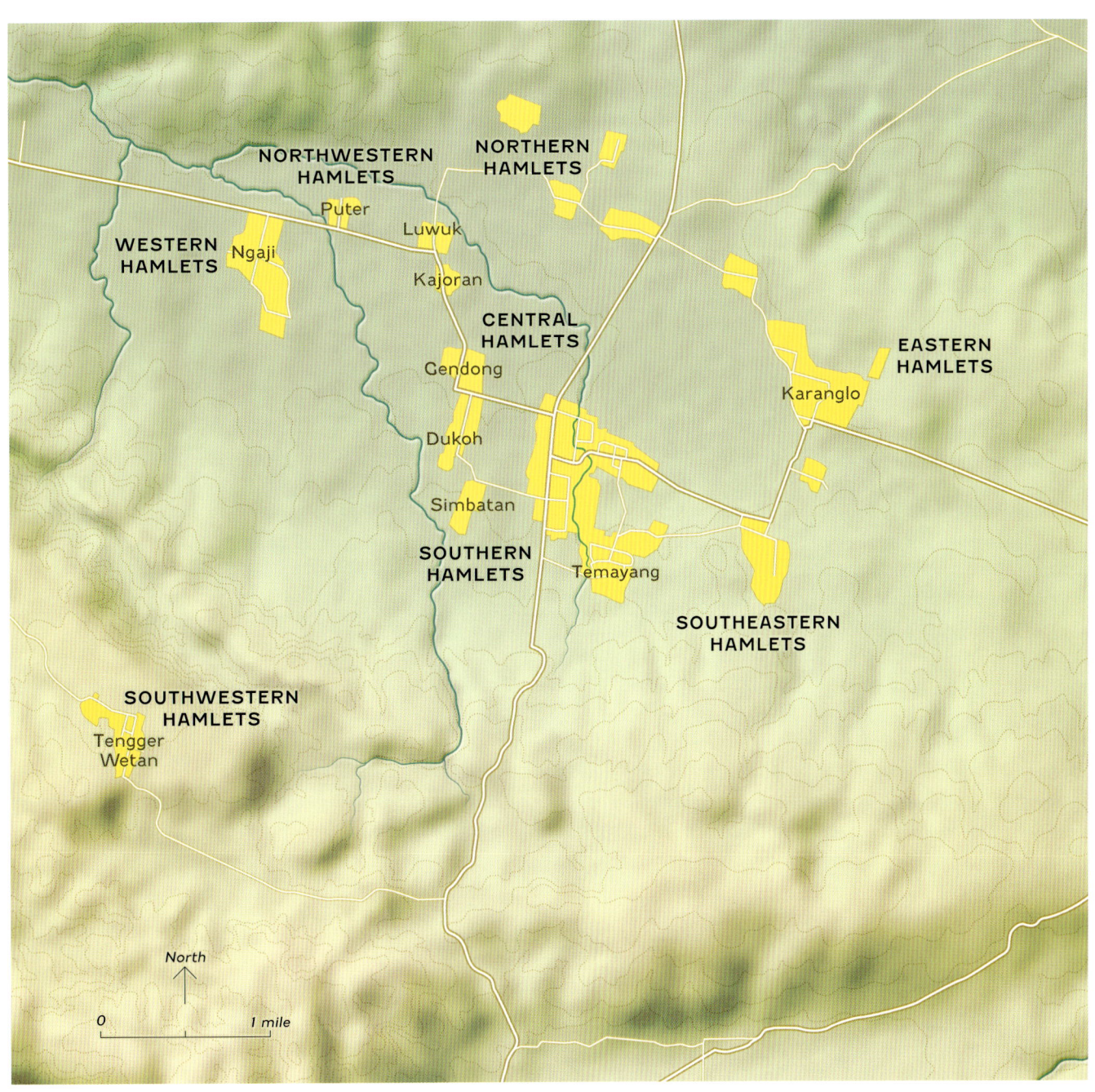

FIGURE 2
The Kerek region with some of the major hamlets indicated.

Dress in Kerek

Traditional dress for a woman consists of a skirt cloth (*jarit, tapeh,* or *sarung*) and a shoulder cloth (*sayut*), which is draped over one shoulder or can be used as a sling for carrying a child or market wares. In the distant past women wore no upper-body garment, but Islamic influence over many centuries has led to the widespread use today of the Javanese blouse (*kelambi*). Because these blouses are tailored from commercial fabric, they are not included in this publication. Most village women wear the blouse only when going out in public. Within the family compound the skirt cloth may be topped with a traditional form of camisole (*kutang*), sometimes still made of locally woven cloth, but elderly women generally just wrap their skirt cloths high over their breasts (a wrapping style known as *pinjungan*). Today most landowners' wives in Kerek store their traditional skirt cloths in the family heirloom chest, only bringing them out for special occasions. Low-quality commercial batiks serve as daily wear, while an Islamic dress and head scarf combination is also gaining influence. Women of the younger generation or from the landless segment of society have recently adopted low-priced flower-print dresses made of synthetic fabrics. The handwoven *sayut*, however, remains an indispensable element in all of these new forms of dress.

For men, the traditional lower-body garment used to be a pair of tailored knee-length pants in a loose Javanese style (*celana kagok*), topped by a tailored jacket of the same fabric. These garments were used especially for semi-official events, and the fabrics employed indicated the man's position. A wider, gusseted style of trousers (*sruwal*), derived from a type originating in Persia, is worn for work on the land, combined with an informal loose-fitting shirt (*baju cina*) nowadays made of shop-bought material. The tubular skirt cloth for men (*sarung amba*) can be worn over the pants for formal occasions, but it is more often carried slung across the chest instead. Although locally handwoven fabrics for men have been almost completely eclipsed by shop-bought cloth, the traditional tailored forms of the garments have endured, as have preferences in color. Handwoven lengths of cloth for male attire continue to be made only for the elite, for whom these cloths remain important as part of the bridal gift.

FIGURE 3
A husband and wife walk toward their fields. The use of commercial garments by the man is typical. The wife wears a commercial batik skirt cloth (*kain tukon*) for work in the fields but uses a locally made batik shoulder cloth (*sayut*) to carry their child. The red *sayut* is considered appropriate for the planting season.
PHOTOGRAPH BY RENS HERINGA, KEREK, 1989.

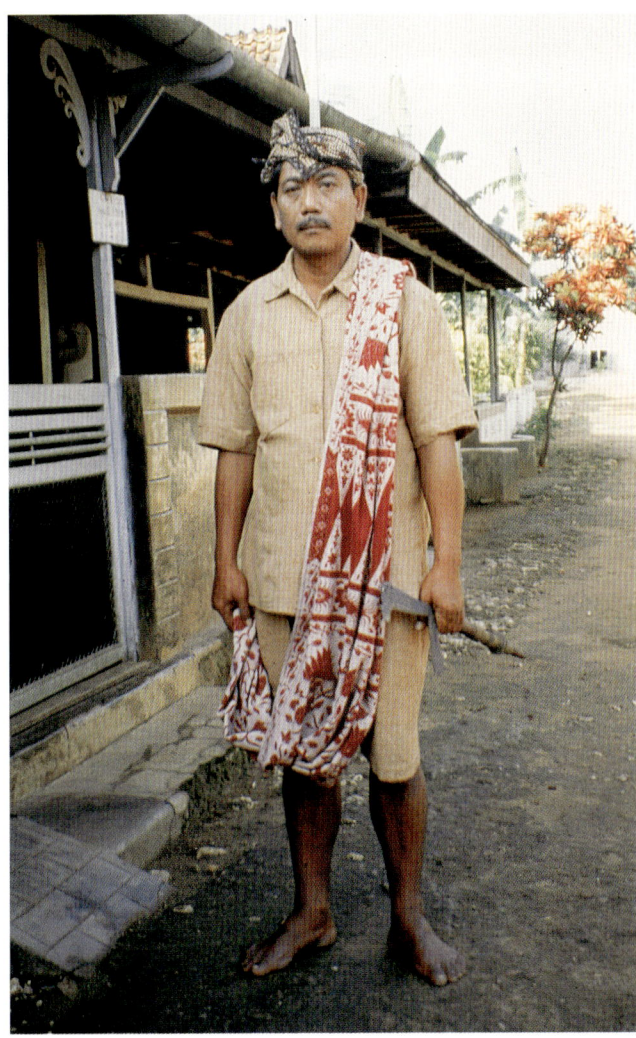

FIGURE 4
Women wear skirt cloths in a variety of informal ways within the family compound. This grandmother wears a neatly bound ikat tube skirt (*sarung talenan*) over her breasts in the *pinjungan* style.
PHOTOGRAPH BY THEO VLAAR, NGAJI (WESTERN HAMLETS), KEREK, 1978.

FIGURE 5
The village chief poses in clothing that represents his status as an elite landowner: knee-length pants (*celana kagok*) and jacket (*kelambi*) of handwoven natural brown cotton, a man's red tube skirt (*sarung amba*) folded and passed over his shoulder, and a commercial batik headcloth. PHOTOGRAPH BY RENS HERINGA, GENDONG (CENTRAL HAMLETS), KEREK, 1990.

FIGURE 6
The woman on the right wears a locally made batik skirt cloth (*jarit*), indicating that she belongs to a high-status family, and a dark blue camisole (*kutang*). She carries her child on her hip in a commercial carrying cloth (*gendongan*). To the left, a woman from a lower-status family wears a *batik lurik* cloth wrapped over her breasts rather carelessly in the *pinjungan* style and held in place with a piece of fabric. The young girl in the flower-print camisole (*kutang*) wears an inexpensive commercial batik skirt cloth (*kain tukon*) that marks her as a member of a landless family of agricultural laborers. The protective cloth wrappings over her stomach indicate first menstruation. PHOTOGRAPH BY THEO VLAAR, GENDONG (CENTRAL HAMLETS), KEREK, 1978.

DRESS IN KEREK   15

FIGURE 7
Women dress more formally when leaving the immediate area of the family compound. This woman from the northwestern hamlets, who is selling papayas and a few skeins of yarn in Kerek's community marketplace, wears a dark red *batik lurik* skirt cloth, a blouse (*kelambi*) of lacy black commercial fabric, and a locally made batik shoulder cloth (*sayut*). PHOTOGRAPH BY RENS HERINGA, KEREK, 1989.

FIGURE 8
The wife of the village smith (right) wears a high-status batik skirt cloth (*jarit*) while hosting a seven-months pregnancy ritual for her son and daughter-in-law. Her daughter-in-law's mother (left) wears a commercial batik skirt cloth (*kain tukon*), indicating her landless status. The lighter coloration of her garments, compared to those of the hostess, also indicates her inferior or "younger" social standing. Both women wear waist sashes (*stagen*). PHOTOGRAPH BY RENS HERINGA, DUKOH (CENTRAL HAMLETS), KEREK, 1989.

FIGURE 9
Village leaders occupy the front row as they gather for a community event—as is done in villages throughout rural Java. They wear several forms of modernized "official" dress. Their tailored shirts show a mixture of locally made batik, with traditional motifs and colors, and the industrially printed imitation batik that is regarded as "national" dress in Indonesia. The black velvet caps (*pici*) also are considered part of the national dress. Some of the women in the back are dressed in Islamic style with head scarves. PHOTOGRAPH BY RENS HERINGA. GENDONG (CENTRAL HAMLETS), KEREK, 1990.

FIGURE 10
These women, leaving the house of the hamlet chief with gifts of food for a senior family member in another hamlet, wear various forms of modernized dress made of commercial fabrics, including one locally batik-dyed tailored skirt. Only one woman, who is more senior, wears a traditional skirt cloth (back right), but all use locally made batik shoulder cloths (*sayut*). PHOTOGRAPH BY RENS HERINGA. GENDONG (CENTRAL HAMLETS), KEREK, 1990.

The Design Formats of Kerek Cloths

The **TAPEH** is a long rectangular skirt cloth for women with woven or ikat patterning (but not batik). As a metaphor for the system of dry-field (*tegal*) agriculture (see fig. 12), the central design field of a *tapeh* is called by the same name as a dry cultivated field (*pelemahan*), while small banks (*galengan*) run along the selvages. The ends of the cloth show a wider border, often in contrasting colors and with a more widely spaced pattern called the *tumpal*, which is said to represent the trees and shrubs at the end of the field. The cloth is wrapped around the body in a clockwise direction, finishing with the end just to the right of center. (For a larger illustration, see cat. no. 3.)

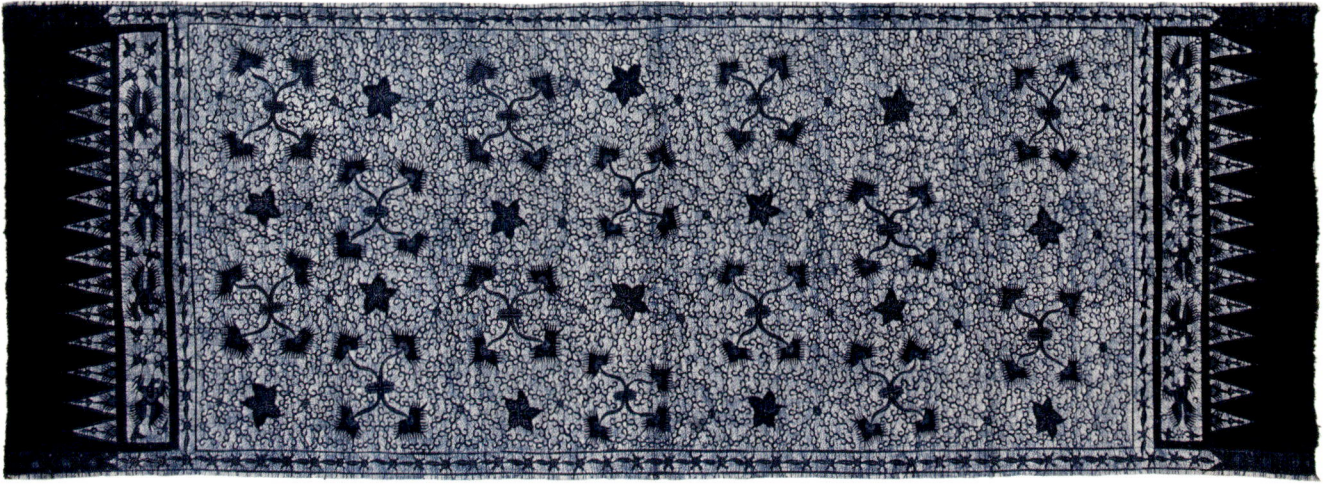

The **JARIT** is a long rectangular batik skirt cloth for women, the design of which metaphorically represents a wet rice field (*sawah*; see fig. 13). It also features a "cultivated field" (*pelemahan*) at the center that is enclosed within a bund or dike (*pinggir*). The borders (*tumpal*) at the two ends comprise the rectangular *bogeman* (sections of the field where special varieties of rice with ritual significance and protective properties are planted) and the row of triangular *pucuk rebung* (bamboo shoots). A dark "drainage ditch" (*glontor*) surrounds the *bogeman*. A *jarit* is wrapped in the same manner as a *tapeh*. (For a larger illustration, see cat. no. 56.)

The **SARUNG** and **SARUNG AMBA** are tubular skirt cloths worn by women and men respectively. The panel(s) of cloth that make up the tubular garment are shorter in length than *tapeh* or *jarit* (roughly 180 cm, as opposed to 220–280 cm). The *tumpal* section is located in the center of the cloth rather than at the two ends. A woman's *sarung* is made of a single panel of cloth, usually with woven patterning (see cat. nos. 24, 36, 50) rather than batik. Once it is sewn into the tubular form, it is about 90 cm in height (the maximum width of a panel of cloth on the loom). Men's *sarung amba* (shown here) are composed of two narrower panels of batik cloth joined together and are therefore somewhat longer than women's *sarung* in total. A woman lowers her *sarung* over her head and neatly folds the *tumpal* in front of her body, whereas a man steps into his *sarung amba* and cinches in the extra material from the two sides, leaving the *tumpal* running down the center of the back. (For a larger illustration, see cat. no. 54.)

A **SISIHAN** cloth has two different patterns in the central design field, one on the left and one on the right. The design format occurs in batik (shown here) and also in woven patterning (see cat. no. 34). By changing the way the cloth is wrapped, the wearer can choose to show one pattern or the other. A batik *jarit sisihan* is comparable to the *pagi-sore* (morning-afternoon) cloth used in other parts of Java, but the two patterns used in a *pagi-sore* are divided diagonally, whereas the division runs perpendicularly across the cloth in a *sisihan*. (For a larger illustration, see cat. no. 10.)

A **BUNTUNGAN** cloth has no *tumpal*, or border, section. *Buntungan* means "chopped off" or "lying fallow." As the *tumpal* is associated with regeneration, a *jarit buntungan* is intended for post-menopausal women. *Buntungan* cloths may also be used as wedding canopies (as with this example) or as funeral shrouds (see cat. no. 64). (For a larger illustration, see cat. no. 33.)

THE DESIGN FORMATS OF KEREK CLOTHS

Land Ownership, Social Class, and Textile Techniques in Kerek

Kerek occupies an infertile pocket of land enclosed by the foothills of the Northern Limestone Mountains some twenty miles inland from Tuban, an old trading port on the Java Sea. The original inhabitants of this area were the Kalang, a people who roamed the forests at least as early as the tenth century and regard themselves as the owners of trees and natural springs. They are therefore generally considered to be guardians of well-being and regeneration. Although they were forced into sedentary life by the seventeenth century, their descendants still show a preference for itinerant lifestyles and keep somewhat aloof from the farming population. Most of Kerek's forests were cleared beginning in the early eighteenth century, and today the hilly and eroded lowlands are mostly covered with scrub. A few scattered groves of teak trees remain around grave sites.

A man may be classed as an owner of agricultural land in Kerek in three different ways: as a *bakalan*, a *tegal*-owner, or a *sawah*-owner. The *bakalan* ("raw" or "original" ones) are the descendants of the community's first settled farmers, recognized as the original owners of the cultivated lands, and the village leadership is preferably drawn from this group. *Tegal* are the most productive dry fields, used primarily for growing maize and tuberous crops, the daily staples. *Sawah*, the most valuable type of land, consists of bunded fields that fill with rainwater at the start of the wet season and are planted with rice, which is grown as a special ceremonial food rather than a daily staple. During the dry season, both *tegal* and *sawah* lands are planted with cotton and indigo as secondary crops. *Sawah* owners comprise Kerek's social elite. The lowest-ranking segment of Kerek society consists of the substantial class of landless commoners, the people who do not own any agricultural land. Some own their houses and the yards (*tanah pekarangan*) that surround them, where a few garden fruits or vegetables can be grown. Others, called *numpang*, rent their dwellings. Those who own no fields typically work as agricultural laborers (*kuli tani*) on land belonging to others in return for a share of the yield.

The women of Kerek create cloth with five different types of patterning, each relying on a separate technique (see pp. 20–29). All of the more highly decorated types of cloth are regarded as the appropriate dress for a particular social group—*lurik talenan* for the *bakalan*, *lurik kembangan* for *tegal* owners, *batik lurik* for the Kalang,

LURIK is patterned only with stripes or checks in plain weave and was formerly considered the appropriate dress for those who owned no agricultural land. Striped *lurik* (with its patterning in the warp) was used for men's garments, especially jackets; while checked *lurik* (with its patterning in the weft as well as the warp) was used for the skirt cloths of their wives.

The cotton yarn in this length of fabric for a man's jacket is thicker than normal because it comes from the hamlet of Tengger Wetan, where the cooler mountain climate calls for warmer garments. The green color, produced with natural dyes, is uncommon in Kerek. Sometimes cloths with unusual color combinations denoted specific ranks within the village leadership. Such traditions persisted longer in Kerek than elswhere in Java. This cloth is a fragment, and it appears that some of it has been cut off in order to fulfill an obligation to include a piece of this type in a *sasrahan*, the betrothal gift made to a son's future bride.

CAT. NO. 2
Detail of fabric for a man's jacket (*bakal kelambi*)

Tengger Wetan (southwestern hamlets), Kerek, East Java, Indonesia, heirloom when collected in 1990. Handspun/handwoven cotton, plain weave. Pattern name: *kulit blungkon* (melon skin). Length 205 cm. PRIVATE COLLECTION.

and batik for *sawah*-owners. The plainest cloth, *lurik*, was once generally regarded as the dress of those who owned only *tanah pekarangan*, although some special forms of *lurik* marked people of certain occupational specializations (see p. 48 and cat. no. 24). Today landless commoners wear store-bought clothing, which includes inexpensive ready-made garments and also commercial batik cloths (*kain tukon*) made outside of Kerek. *Kain tukon* is available in different qualities and in addition to comprising the dress of the landless class (see figs. 6, 8), it also serves as daily work wear for women of all classes (see fig. 3) and for other special purposes (see fig. 21, cat. nos. 27, 47).

These relationships are most readily seen today in the skirt cloths of married women, while women of all social classes wear batik shoulder cloths. Similar principles once applied to men's clothing as well, but these are less easily observed today due to the widespread adoption of store-bought fabric for men's clothing.

FIGURE 11
Women come to bathe and to wash their laundry in a natural mountain spring that flows from among the roots of a giant tree—remnant of the primary forest regarded as the domain of the Kalang. PHOTOGRAPH BY RENS HERINGA, NEAR SOCO (A SOUTHWESTERN HAMLET), KEREK, 1990.

FIGURE 12
The landowner's son scatters fertilizer behind the plow in a dry field (*tegal*), while women drop seed corn into the furrows, covering it with a quick movement of the foot. The land is the hamlet chief's heirloom field (*tanah pusaka*). PHOTOGRAPH BY RENS HERINGA, GENDONG (CENTRAL HAMLETS), KEREK, 1989.

FIGURE 13
Men scatter rice seed in a bunded field (*sawah*), which was plowed a second time once it filled with rainwater when the monsoon season broke. PHOTOGRAPH BY RENS HERINGA, GENDONG (CENTRAL HAMLETS), KEREK, 1989.

LURIK TALENAN has patterning made with the ikat resist-dye process. The patterns are limited to simple white and bright blue dotted lines in the warp—or to cross-hatches in the case of compound ikat, in which ikat yarns are used for both warp and weft. Warp ikat cloth is intended for men, whereas compound ikat cloth is for women. Kerek ikat cloth never has the elaborate patterns found in examples from most other areas in the archipelago, as the ikat bindings are simply tied directly into skeins of yarn with strips of corn husk, rather than using a tying-frame. *Lurik talenan* cloth is appropriate dress for the *bakalan*, or descendants of the original cultivators of the land in Kerek, the group from which the village leadership is still chosen today.

FIGURE 14
A woman ties ikat bindings, using strips of corn husks, directly onto a skein of white handspun cotton yarn. PHOTOGRAPH BY THEO VLAAR, NGAJI (WESTERN HAMLETS), KEREK, 1978.

The unusually bright red selvages and *tumpal*, or border, sections suggest that this cloth was made in the eastern hamlets. The pattern name *merang bodhol* refers to rice straw strewn on the field to serve as fertilizer after the harvest. The dark pattern is therefore worn by post-menopausal women.

CAT. NO. 3
Woman's rectangular skirt cloth (*tapeh*)

Karanglo (eastern hamlets), Kerek, East Java, Indonesia, heirloom when collected in 1989. Handspun/handwoven cotton, plain weave with compound ikat. Pattern name: *merang bodhol*. Length 260 cm.
PRIVATE COLLECTION.

The skein of yarn on the left has been prepared for dyeing by being bound with small strips of corn husk into a series of lozenges. After being dyed with indigo and having the bindings removed, the yarn on the right is bright blue with white markings where the ties have prevented the dye from penetrating. The weaver of the *lurik talenan* cloth (cat. no. 3) has used this kind of yarn for both the warp and weft of the cloth, creating a checked or cross-hatched pattern.

CAT. NO. 4A,B
Detail of skeins of ikat yarn before and after dyeing

Gendong (central hamlets), Kerek, East Java, Indonesia, 1989. Handspun cotton yarn (*lawai*), corn husk. PRIVATE COLLECTION.

DETAIL OF CAT. NO. 3

LURIK KEMBANGAN has tiny "floral" motifs woven into it (*kembang* means "blossom" in Javanese). This type of cloth is reserved for the use of men who are the owners of the most productive dry agricultural lands (*tegal*) and their wives. If the motifs are created in the warp using a warp-float weave, the cloth is for a man. If they are created in the weft using the supplementary-weft technique, as in the cloth illustrated here, it is intended for a woman.

Most wives of *tegal* owners use handspun cotton yarn for warp-float weaves and buy fine industrial yarn in the market for supplementary weft. In former times, wives of the village leaders chose yellow or white silk yarns imported from China in order to signal the rank of their husbands. Later, mercerized cotton yarns from Europe were substituted. Today some use imitation metallic yarn in gold or silver, but the older generation frowns upon this gaudy and ostentatious effect.

CAT. NO. 5
Woman's skirt cloth with silk supplementary-weft yarn (*tapeh benang sutera*)

Kerek, East Java, Indonesia, circa 1910. Handspun/handwoven cotton, with silk supplementary weft. Pattern name: *ksatriyan*. Length 270 cm. X2008.26.18; GIFT OF MARY JANE LELAND.

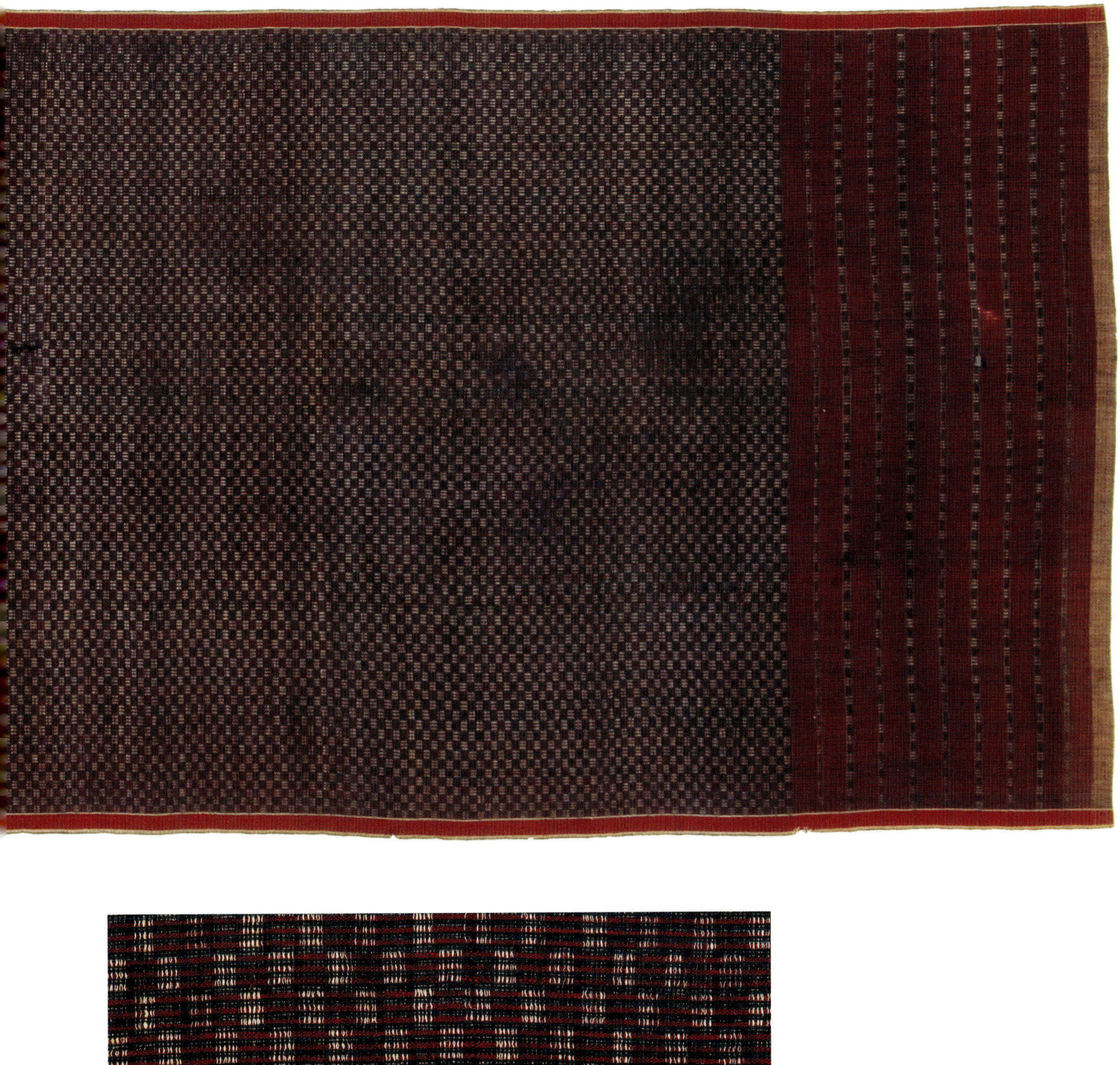

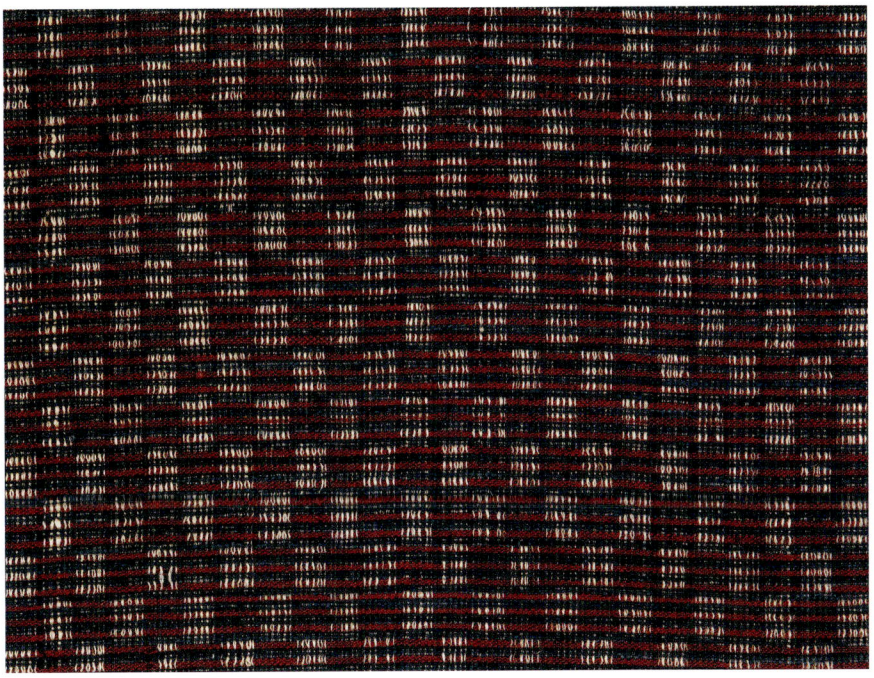

DETAIL OF CAT. NO. 5

LAND OWNERSHIP, SOCIAL CLASS, AND TEXTILE TECHNIQUES IN KEREK

BATIK LURIK is a hybrid of *lurik* and batik (see pp. 28–29), and the people of Kerek acknowledge it as their earliest decorative technique other than plain *lurik* weaving. A *batik lurik* cloth starts as a checked piece of *lurik*, which is then used as a grid on which to make simple dotted batik patterns. In the past *batik lurik* may have been waxed using just a finely split piece of bamboo—suggesting it might indeed represent an archaic form of batik. Until the mid-nineteenth century, it was made throughout East and Central Java. Large numbers of imported Dutch industrial imitations contributed to the decline of the technique around 1870. Today *batik lurik* is made only in Kerek, and the molten wax is applied, as on ordinary batik, using a special tool called a *canting* (see cat. no. 9).

In Kerek *batik lurik* is the appropriate dress for the Kalang, the people who still consider themselves to be the descendants of the original forest inhabitants of the area even though they were forced long ago to settle in villages.

CAT. NO. 6
Woman's skirt cloth (*tapeh*)

Gendong (central hamlets), Kerek, East Java, Indonesia, 1984. Batik on handspun/handwoven cotton *lurik*. Color combination: *biron*. Pattern name: *kembang pepe* (blossoms of *Oxystelma esculentum*). Length 247 cm. X2008.10.11; PURCHASED BY FOWLER MUSEUM TEXTILE COUNCIL.

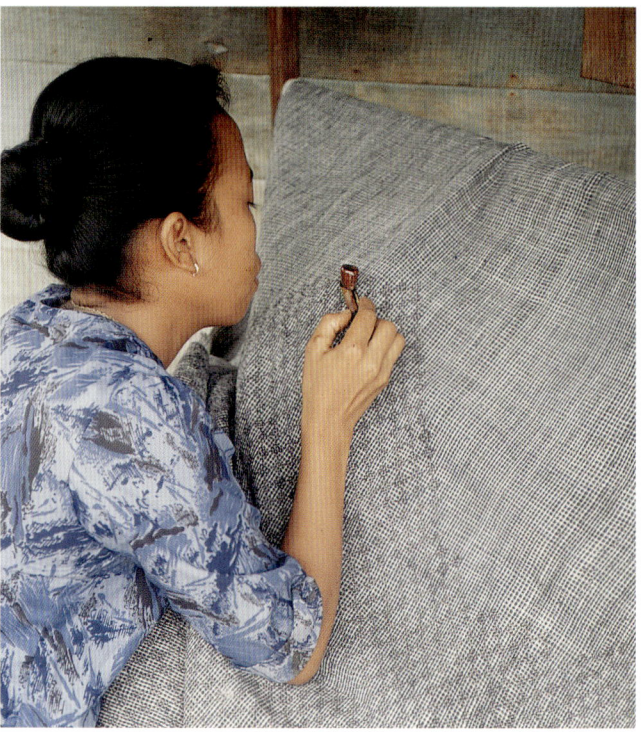

FIGURE 15
A woman applies wax to a *lurik* base cloth to make *batik lurik*.
PHOTOGRAPH BY RENS HERINGA, NGAJI (WESTERN HAMLETS), KEREK, 1989.

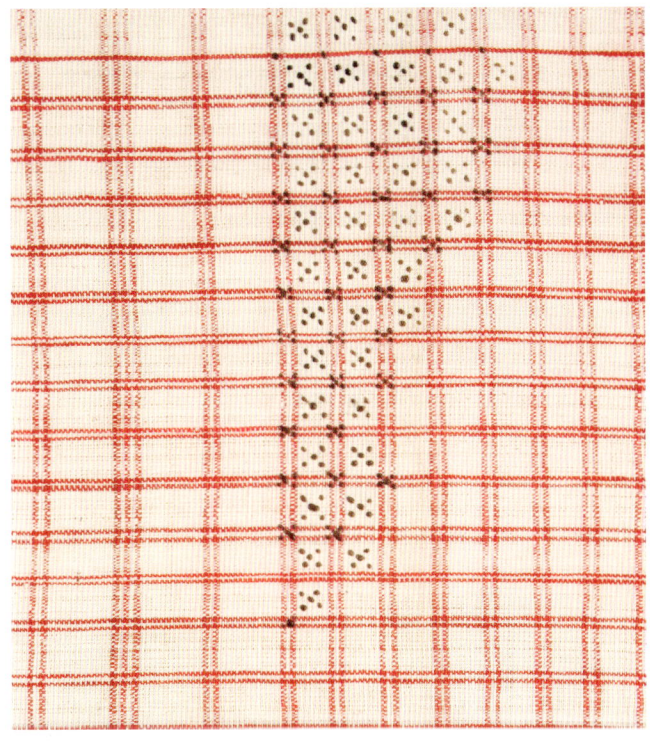

CAT. NO. 7
Detail of partially waxed base cloth
(*kotongan*, "empty body") for making *batik lurik*

Ngaji (western hamlets), Kerek, East Java, Indonesia, 1979.
Handspun/handwoven cotton, partially waxed. Length 270 cm.
PRIVATE COLLECTION.

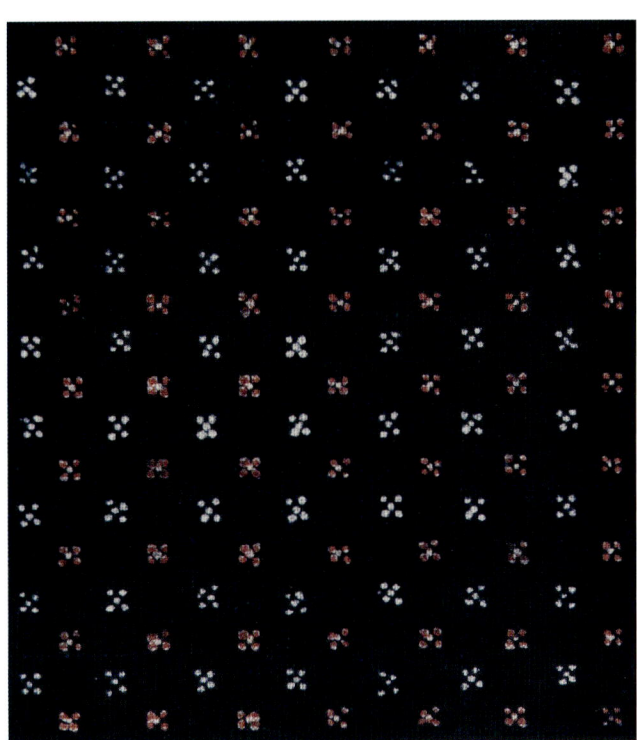

DETAIL OF CAT. NO. 6

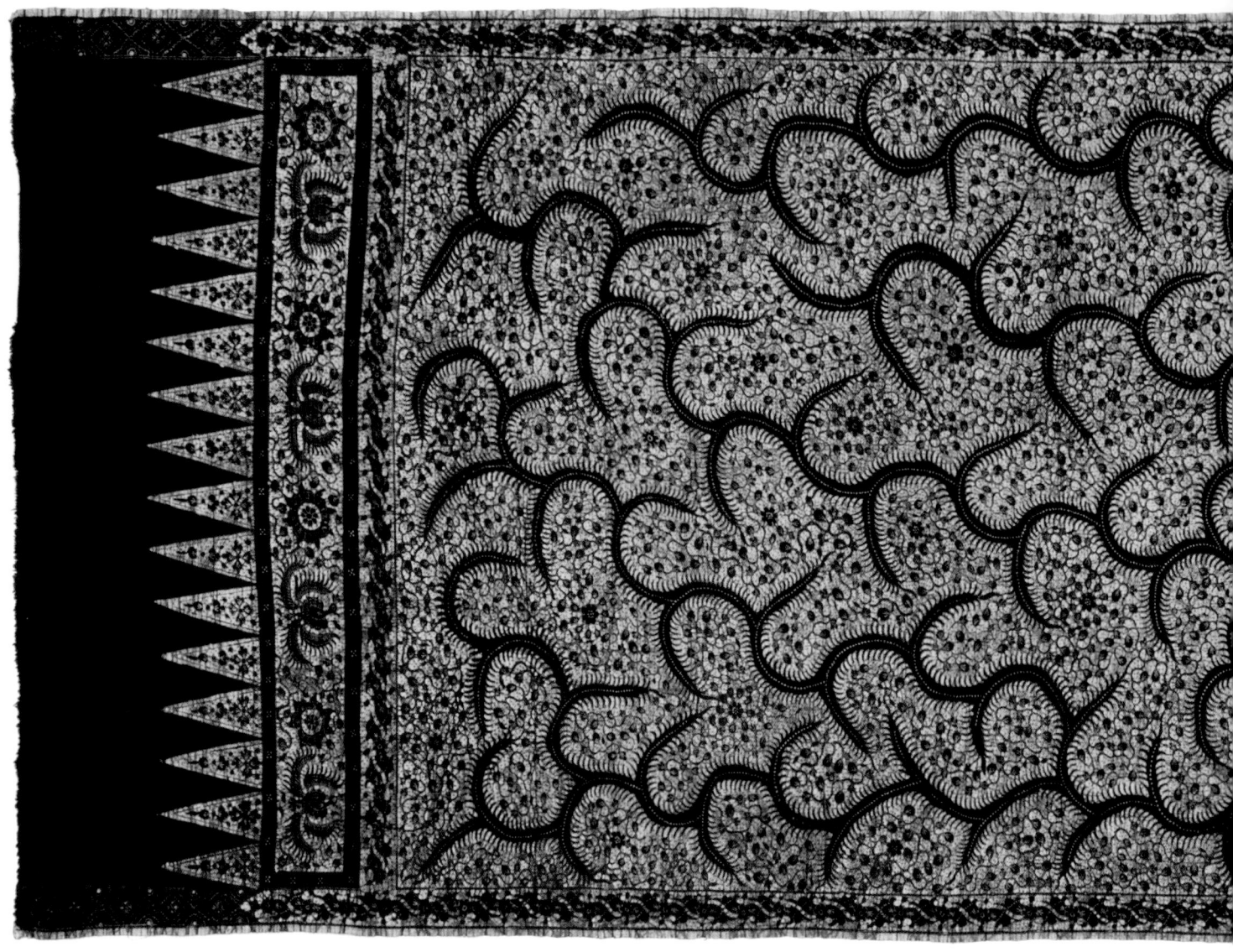

BATIK features elaborate motifs created entirely with the wax-resist dye process on plain white fabric. In Kerek the wax is always applied freehand with a tool known as a *canting* (see cat. no. 9). If intended for local use, it is almost always made on handspun/handwoven cotton cloth. Women of all social groups wear batik shoulder cloths. Batik skirt cloths, however, are reserved for the wives of the elite men who own *sawah* land.

CAT. NO. 8

Woman's skirt cloth (*jarit*)

Gendong (central hamlets), Kerek, East Java, Indonesia, 1989. Batik on handspun/handwoven cotton. Color combination: *irengan*. Pattern name: *kelabang melaku* (wandering centipede). Length 250 cm. X2008.10.21; PURCHASED BY FOWLER MUSEUM TEXTILE COUNCIL.

The copper reservoir of the *canting* holds molten wax, which flows through the narrow spout onto the surface of the cloth.

CAT. NO. 9
Canting

Java, Indonesia, late twentieth century. Copper, bamboo. Length 13.5 cm. X2000.20.6; GIFT OF PAUL POLAKOFF.

FIGURE 16
Embah Asih, one of Kerek's most skilled batik makers, blows on her *canting* to cool it, controlling the viscosity of the wax. She is working on cat. no. 49. She is also the maker of cat. nos. 8 and 56. PHOTOGRAPH BY RENS HERINGA, GENDONG (CENTRAL HAMLETS), KEREK, 1990.

The Patterning of Batik Cloth: Floral or Abstract

Two different styles of patterning are found in Kerek batik. The first style, floral patterning, occurs in a variety of color combinations and always consists of relatively dark motifs against a lighter ground. Various forms of floral creepers tend to predominate. Bird motifs are commonly added to shoulder cloths but not to the main design fields in skirt cloths (although they can be found in the borders). When they appear together, the floral and bird images have a cosmological significance representing the life forms of land and sky.

Abstract patterning, the second style, is more geometric, usually appearing in the form of thin white lines on a dark ground. More rarely, abstract motifs appear in dark blue on a white ground. The abstract motifs are visually related to cosmic models that occur in designs found throughout Southeast Asia, including Hindu-Buddhist mandalas or comparable designs on imported Indian trade cloths. While both floral and abstract designs are suitable for dress and for ritual, the abstract cloths always have the higher status.

FLORAL PATTERNS appear in the main design field of this skirt cloth, one on the left side and a contrasting one on the right. Cloths with a field divided in this manner are called *sisihan* (with different sides). The pattern on the right is *kembang waluh* (flowers of the bottle gourd), a plant that is much cultivated in the northwestern and northern hamlets. The pattern on the left is *ganggeng*, the aquatic weed (*Hydrilla verticillata*) that trails through inundated rice fields. A fusion of floral and bird motifs appears in the rectangular *bogeman* section in the borders of this cloth.

The northwestern and northern hamlets are rich in ponds, making it easy to grow garden crops, and their residents are customarily expected to contribute various vegetal condiments to community feasts. The borders of this cloth show one of these condiments, the tasty basil (*semanggi*) leaves that frequently appear in northwestern and northern batik patterns.

CAT. NO. 10
Woman's skirt cloth (*jarit sisihan*)

Puter (northwestern hamlets), Kerek, East Java, Indonesia, heirloom when collected in 1989. Batik on handspun/handwoven cotton. Color combination: *pipitan*. Pattern names: *kembang waluh, ganggeng*. Length 284 cm. X2008.10.19; PURCHASED BY FOWLER MUSEUM TEXTILE COUNCIL.

DETAIL OF CAT. NO. 10

THE PATTERNING OF BATIK CLOTH: FLORAL OR ABSTRACT 31

ABSTRACT PATTERNS are found primarily on skirt cloths for elderly men and women. The patterns are commonly built up from at least two abstracted floral elements that cover the central field in a structured layer. In Kerek, these patterns are conceived of as representing three-dimensional structures (comparable to an aerial view of buildings or landscape). As such, they become models for cosmic dualities such as land and water or land and sky. Ordinary floral patterns are not interpreted in this way.

The pattern of this cloth, *kemiri kobong* ("burnt candlenut," *Aleurites moluccana*) is associated with a range of cultural ideas. Treating the cotton yarn with candlenut oil was once an essential step in the morinda dyeing process, said to make the red "smile" properly. Burnt candlenuts were used to clean metallic weapons (*caluk*) and to make a woman's hair darker and shiny. Though seemingly mundane, all of these activities have in common the enhancement of appearance and an increase in efficacy.

CAT. NO. 11
Woman's skirt cloth (*jarit*)

Possibly Gendong (central hamlets), Kerek, East Java, Indonesia, first half of twentieth century. Batik on handspun/handwoven cotton cloth. Color combination: *irengan*. Pattern name: *kemiri kobong*. Length 274 cm. X2008.26.24; GIFT OF MARY JANE LELAND.

DETAIL OF CAT. NO. 11

THE PATTERNING OF BATIK CLOTH: FLORAL OR ABSTRACT

Color in Kerek Batiks

The colors of a Kerek batik provide one of the most important keys to understanding the messages that the cloth communicates regarding the identity of the wearer. Most cloths fall into one of five common named color combinations (as illustrated and discussed in the examples that follow). Red tones were formerly dyed with morinda (*mengkudu* in Javanese), a natural dye produced from the inner bark of the roots of trees of the genus *Morinda*. Since the 1970s, however, morinda has been replaced with synthetic naphthol dyes (see p. 80). Natural indigo (*nila*) is still used in the highest-quality cloths for blue and blue-black tones. Only rarely do batiks show touches of other colors such as yellow, green, or purple.

PUTIHAN cloths are produced using indigo alone. The bright blue motifs appear on a white ground dotted with tiny blue *coblosan* (lit., "pinpricked") made in the waxed background. In Kerek, *putihan* cloths are considered to be "otherworldly" as they are associated with the northeast, the direction of the compass that is poised between death and regeneration. The term *putihan* itself means "whitened" or "purified," referring to the cloth's special protective properties rather than to its color.

Putihan shoulder cloths are thus not worn like cloths in the other color combinations, which indicate the stages of a woman's life. Instead they have a more specific function. When a woman gives birth to her first child, her mother-in-law presents her with a *putihan* shoulder cloth to use as a sling for carrying her baby. The mother-in-law herself is regarded as somewhat "otherworldly," having come into the community from outside due to the virilocal marriage pattern, wherein a bride goes to live with the family of her new husband. The cloth is washed as little as possible in order to keep its protective powers intact. When the child is older, the cloth may be used as a wrap in time of illness.

CAT. NO. 12
Woman's shoulder cloth (*sayut*)

Gendong (central hamlets), Kerek, East Java, Indonesia, heirloom when collected in 1996. Batik on handspun/handwoven cotton cloth. Color combination: *putihan*. Pattern name: *laseman*. Width 57 cm. X2008.10.16; PURCHASED BY FOWLER MUSEUM TEXTILE COUNCIL.

The background pattern of this *putihan* shoulder cloth is a village version of the diagonal *parang* (machete) pattern. The overlay of roundels consists of rows of three, a reference to three generations living together in the family house.

CAT. NO. 13
Woman's shoulder cloth (*sayut*)

Possibly Gendong (central hamlets), Kerek, East Java, Indonesia, prior to 1940. Batik on handspun/handwoven cotton cloth. Color combination: *putihan*. Pattern name: *lereng* (diagonal). Width 55 cm.
X2002.37.80; GIFT OF E. M. BAKWIN.

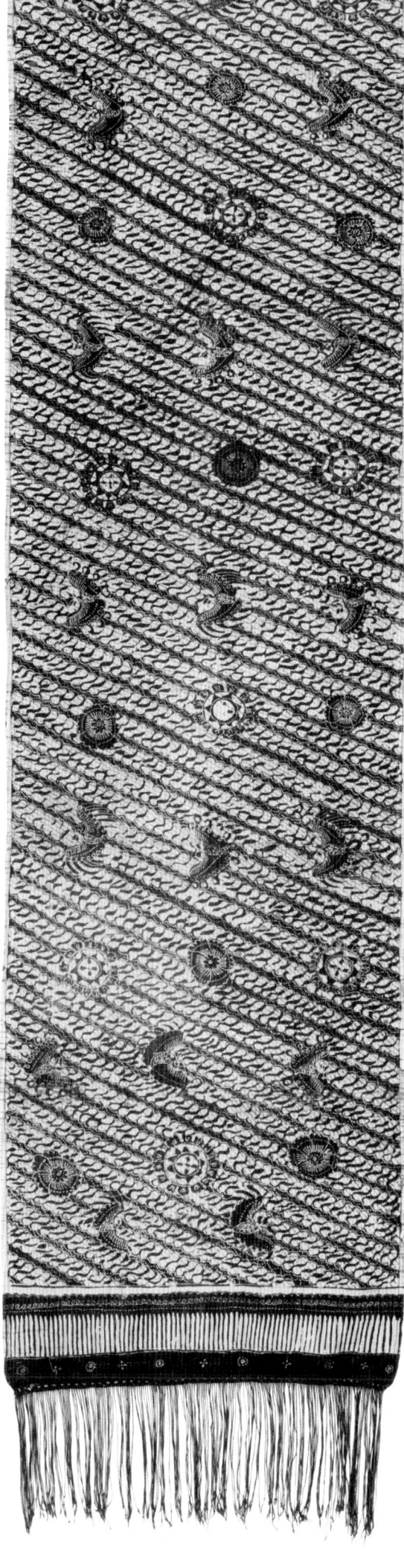

This *putihan* shoulder cloth bears a rare, archaic pattern that would be unfamiliar to many batik artists. It was made by the daughter of Kerek's main cloth trader, who has access to rare cloths to use as models. As she is missing a finger, the young woman is considered unmarriageable. This misfortune has, however, allowed her to devote her time to the making of fine batik even though she is not from the most elite group in the central hamlets, who are categorically regarded as the most accomplished batik artists.

The pattern *lar wonga* (winged bosom) depicts "birds" with an unusual degree of abstraction, which suggests a deeper symbolic meaning. Pairs of birds, visualized as two interconnected pairs of wings, hover over the undulating swampy waters (*rawan*) of the background. The six squares combined into a triangular form have Chinese, and possibly Islamic, connotations. Painted on the upper side walls of the fifteenth-century seaside Chinese temple (*klenteng*) in Tuban town, this motif is believed to express a wish for peace and tranquility.

CAT. NO. 14
Woman's shoulder cloth (*sayut*)

Ngaji (western hamlets), Kerek, East Java, Indonesia, 1980s. Batik on handspun/handwoven cotton cloth. Color combination: *putihan*. Pattern name: *lar wonga*. Width 53 cm. PRIVATE COLLECTION.

BANGROD cloths also use a single dye, but red rather than blue. The red motifs appear on a white ground dotted with red *coblosan* (lit., "pinpricked"). *Bangrod* is a contraction of the terms *diabang* (reddened) and *dilorod* ("boiled," referring to the boiling of the cloth to remove the wax). Because the dyeing process is halted with this boiling, without the cloth being dyed a second color, the cloth is considered "half-done" in local ideology. *Bangrod* cloths are therefore associated with beginnings or regeneration, and they are most prominently seen as shoulder cloths for young women of marriageable age or for a young father when he buries the afterbirth of a new baby near the back door of the house.

This *bangrod* shoulder cloth features the small motifs typical of the eastern hamlets, befitting their "junior" status among the Kerek hamlet clusters. The clear, bright red color is also characteristic of the east.

CAT. NO. 15
Woman's shoulder cloth (*sayut*)

Karanglo (eastern hamlets), Kerek, East Java, Indonesia, 2004. Batik on handspun/handwoven cotton cloth. Color combination: *bangrod*. Pattern: *laseman*. Width 60 cm. PRIVATE COLLECTION.

PIPITAN cloths require two dye colors, one for red and one for blue. In the finished cloth, motifs in red, blue, and black appear on a light ground scattered with blue *coblosan*. After an initial dyeing with red, the red motifs are partially rewaxed and the *coblosan* are pierced into the waxed background. Several steepings in the indigo vat follow, after which the wax is removed by boiling. Black motifs are formed where the red has been left unwaxed and overdyed with indigo. The red and blue colors may appear in bright or dark shades.

These cloths are suitable attire for the middle generation, most typically women with young children. *Pipitan* means "close together" in Javanese, which is regarded as a reference to the ties among a wife, her husband, and their children. The way in which the two dye colors fuse to make a new color is also likened to the relationship between husband and wife.

CAT. NO. 16

Woman's shoulder cloth (*sayut*)

Gendong (central hamlets), Kerek, East Java, Indonesia, early 1980s. Batik on handspun/handwoven cotton cloth. Color combination: *pipitan*. Pattern name: *laseman*. Width 57 cm. PRIVATE COLLECTION.

BIRON (bluish) cloths, like *putihan* cloths, are dyed with indigo alone, but the blue is darker due to additional immersions in the dye vat. Blue *coblosan* dot the background. These cloths are suitable attire for mothers approaching middle age.

Though they are rarely made today, *biron* cloths are still needed to fill the *grobog*, a wooden chest on wheels filled with up to a hundred cloths of all types, for inclusion in the *sasrahan*, the gift from the kin of the groom to the bride, which is presented one week before the wedding to "entice" her to take up residence with the groom in the household of his father.

The same *biron* dye process can be used to create abstract patterns that show the "opposite" color combination in the finished cloth, with light motifs on a blue ground rather than blue motifs on a light ground (see cat. no. 46). Since the dyeing process is the same, these cloths too are called *biron*—the difference is in the waxing.

CAT. NO. 17

Woman's shoulder cloth (*sayut*)

Ngaji (western hamlets), Kerek, East Java, Indonesia, 2000. Batik on handspun/handwoven cotton cloth. Color combination: *biron*. Pattern name: *laseman*. Width 55 cm. PRIVATE COLLECTION.

IRENGAN are the darkest of the Kerek batiks, and feature black motifs on a marbled blue ground dotted with black *coblosan*. After the pattern is waxed, the cloth is immersed repeatedly in indigo. Then, without any rewaxing, the cloth is immersed in a secondary dye to further darken the color. This dye may be either *sogo tingi*, derived from the tannin-rich bark of a mangrove (*kayu tingi*; *Bruguiera* sp.), which yields a somewhat brownish sheen, or *becek*, iron-rich *sawah* mud, which produces a more saturated black. The motifs in the finished cloth, which have been purposefully exposed to both dyes, usually appear darker than the blue marbling in the ground, which is due to the uncontrollable seeping of the dyes through random cracking in the wax. While *sogo tingi* by itself is regarded as a red-brown dye, in *irengan* cloths it never appears by itself, and there are no red motifs in the finished cloth (unlike *pipitan* cloths).

The *irengan* dye process is also used to create cloths with light abstract motifs on a dark ground. The word *irengan* means "blackened" and also "lying fallow after the harvest." The cloths darkened with *sogo tingi* are especially suitable for grandmothers or post-menopausal women. The *irengan* cloths blackened with mud dye are used as funeral shrouds.

While *irengan* cloths are categorically associated with elderly women, they are also (as will be seen in the pages ahead) associated with the northern hamlets, and even a young woman from these hamlets might wear one. The appropriateness of any cloth in Kerek for a particular purpose is judged by multiple categorical standards.

CAT. NO. 18
Woman's shoulder cloth (*sayut*)

Gendong (central hamlets), Kerek, East Java, Indonesia, 1984. Batik on handspun/handwoven cotton cloth. Color combination: *irengan*. Pattern name: *laseman*. Width 53 cm. PRIVATE COLLECTION.

Nini Towok's Spinning Wheel

Elderly people versed in Kerek's oral traditions say that a field of ripened cotton, with its countless bolls bursting open to reveal gleaming white fiber, resembles the night sky dotted with stars. In the markings on the surface of the full moon, they point out an old woman, Nini Towok (Granny Sunken Eyes/Hollow Cheeks), working at her spinning wheel. Part goddess, part crone, Nini Towok sends her finely spun cotton yarn to earth in the form of moonbeams.

With tousled hair like the tangled fibers in a cotton boll, she is also called Nini Dhiwut, or "Granny Shaggy Hair." Prone to abrupt outbursts, she is sometimes described by Kerek men as "too hot" or "unruly." When she died, she was refused burial in the earth. Instead she ascended a *jambe* tree (*Areca catechu*, the "betel nut" palm), whose wood is used for making parts of the loom, and then flew off shrieking toward the moon. Today she tends her cotton fields in the sky.

Nini Towok's "moonbeams" are the most basic material from which the weavers of Kerek fashion their cloth. Nini Towok is their guardian spirit, presiding over the production of cloth, encouraging and admonishing as needed. At the beginning of the weaving process, Kerek women make an offering to her in her guise as a formal Hindu-Javanese deity, Bagendho Ngalih (Her Majesty Who Changes Form).

Nini Towok is thus the initiator of the entire system of textiles with all of its associated meanings. For cloth does not stand alone in Kerek. Rather, it is part of a complex system of knowledge that interconnects many aspects of life and society.

KEREK FARMER'S PRAYER FOR PLANTING COTTON SEEDS

Bismilla'llah Irochmani Rochim. — In the name of Allah, most Gracious, most Compassionate

Niyat ingsun nanem kapas, — My intention is to plant cotton,
Gimbal kaya temlaka, — Sticking together like a *kemlaka* tree,
Mrental kaya keduya, — Curling like the *keduya* plant,
Jerbobok kaya srengenge, — Indeed heavy and full like the sun,
Abior kaya lintang rembulan. — Twinkling like the stars and the moon.
Aja rontok rontok kapas iku — Don't pluck this cotton off the tree
Nek durung rontog lintang rembulan. — If the moon and the stars have not yet set.

Ayo, Ayo sangking Allah — All comes, All comes from Allah.
Ayo, Ayo sangking Allah — All comes, All comes from Allah.
Ayo, Ayo sangking Allah — All comes, All comes from Allah.

CAT. NO. 19
Spinning wheel (*jantra*)

Gendong (central hamlets), Kerek, East Java, Indonesia, 1960s. Teak wood, cotton rags. Length 87 cm. X2010.5.1A–F; GIFT OF RENS HERINGA.

CAT. NO. 20A–C
Bolls of cotton (*kapas puteh mentah*) in a lontar leaf basket (*kepek*)
Handspun white cotton yarn (*lawai puteh mentah*).

Kerek, East Java, Indonesia. X2010.5.5, X2010.5.6; GIFT OF RENS HERINGA.

Nini Towok, the Cardinal Directions, and the Cycles of Color and Life

A Kerek cloth bears many interrelated meanings simultaneously. On one level, it relates to the cardinal directions and in particular to the relative locations of the various hamlets within Kerek. Each group of hamlets has its own distinctive variants of textile designs and practices. The hamlets themselves, as well as their textiles, are metaphorically related to one another from youngest to eldest, progressing around the points of the compass clockwise from the east to the north and finally terminating in the center (see fig. 17). Sets of dress presented on pages 46–79 are arranged according to the locations of the hamlets in which they would be used. Often the cloths were made in those hamlets as well, although in some cases they were ordered from other hamlets that specialize in producing the required type of cloth.

In Kerek's ideological system of color combinations for batik, the colors are also seen as progressing clockwise around the compass beginning with red in the east. The red slowly darkens as it progresses through the southeast, where a pale shade of blue first appears to mingle with it. Moving toward the southwest, a fleeting trace of yellow appears in some red batiks, while darkening shades of red and blue together continue to play the predominant roles progressing toward the west. Between west and north, the dark red is gradually subsumed by deep blue, which darkens to black approaching north.

Thus the people of Kerek categorically associate *putihan* cloth (white and blue) with the area between north and east, *bangrod* cloth (white and red) darkening from the east to the south, *pipitan* cloth (red and blue mixed) with the southwest and west, and *biron* and *irengan* cloths (darkening shades of blue to black) with the northwest and the north respectively (see fig. 19).

Metaphorically speaking, Nini Towok's spinning also sets in motion the cycle of life. Her abode in the northeast is poised midway between the north (associated with death) and the east (associated with regeneration). Just as the colors progress from east around to north, life is said to begin in the east, pass through ever increasing maturity in the south and west, and end with old age and death in the north (see fig. 18).

All of these ideas work simultaneously in underpinning the patterns of dress in Kerek. A fertile young bride-to-be living in the southern hamlets, for example, wears the brightest red shoulder cloth. No one in Kerek would ordinarily express this idealized model in its entirety, yet the underlying principles are intuitively reflected in the daily choices of traditional dress. On pages 46–79, dress items are arranged not only according to the proper hamlet locations but also in a manner that follows the meanings they bear for the people of Kerek with regard to the cycles of color and life.

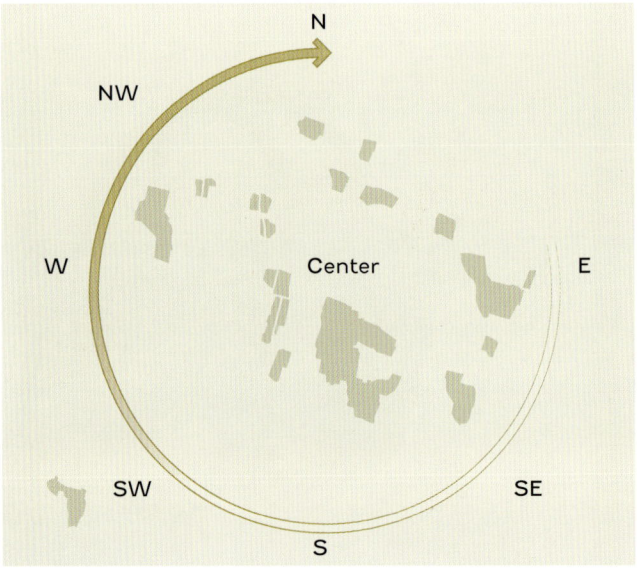

FIGURE 17
This diagram schematically represents the relationships of the Kerek hamlets to each other and to the cardinal directions, which are in turn linked to stages in the life cycle (see fig. 18).

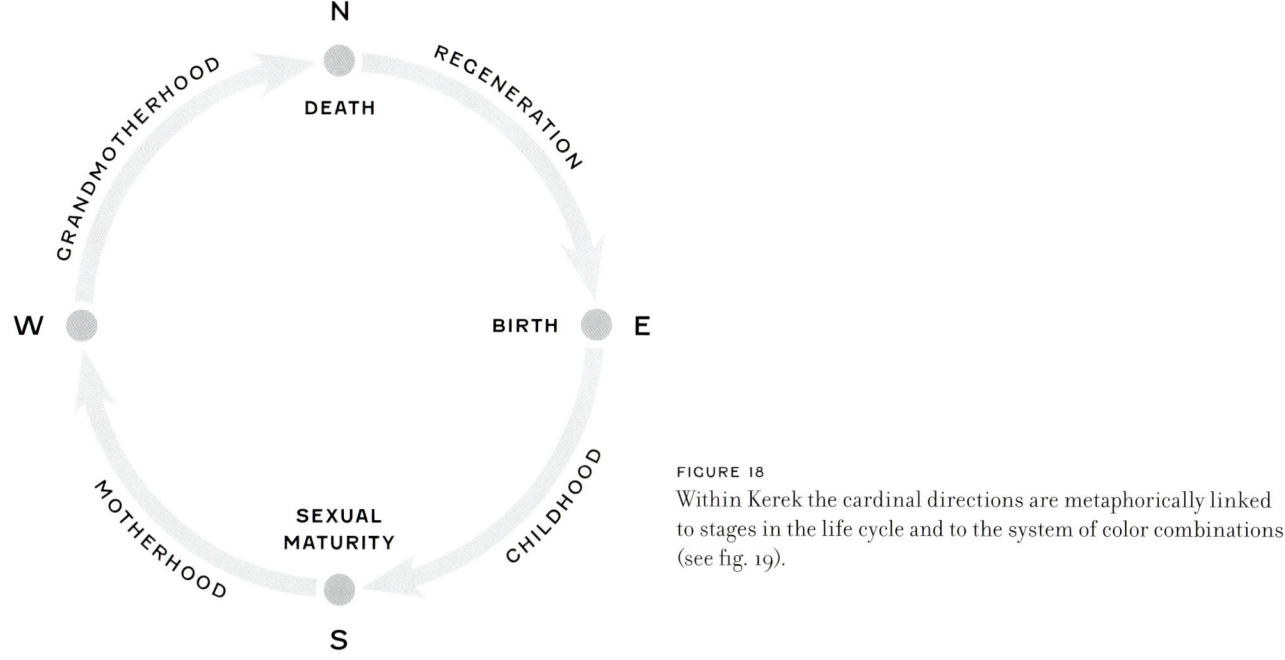

FIGURE 18
Within Kerek the cardinal directions are metaphorically linked to stages in the life cycle and to the system of color combinations (see fig. 19).

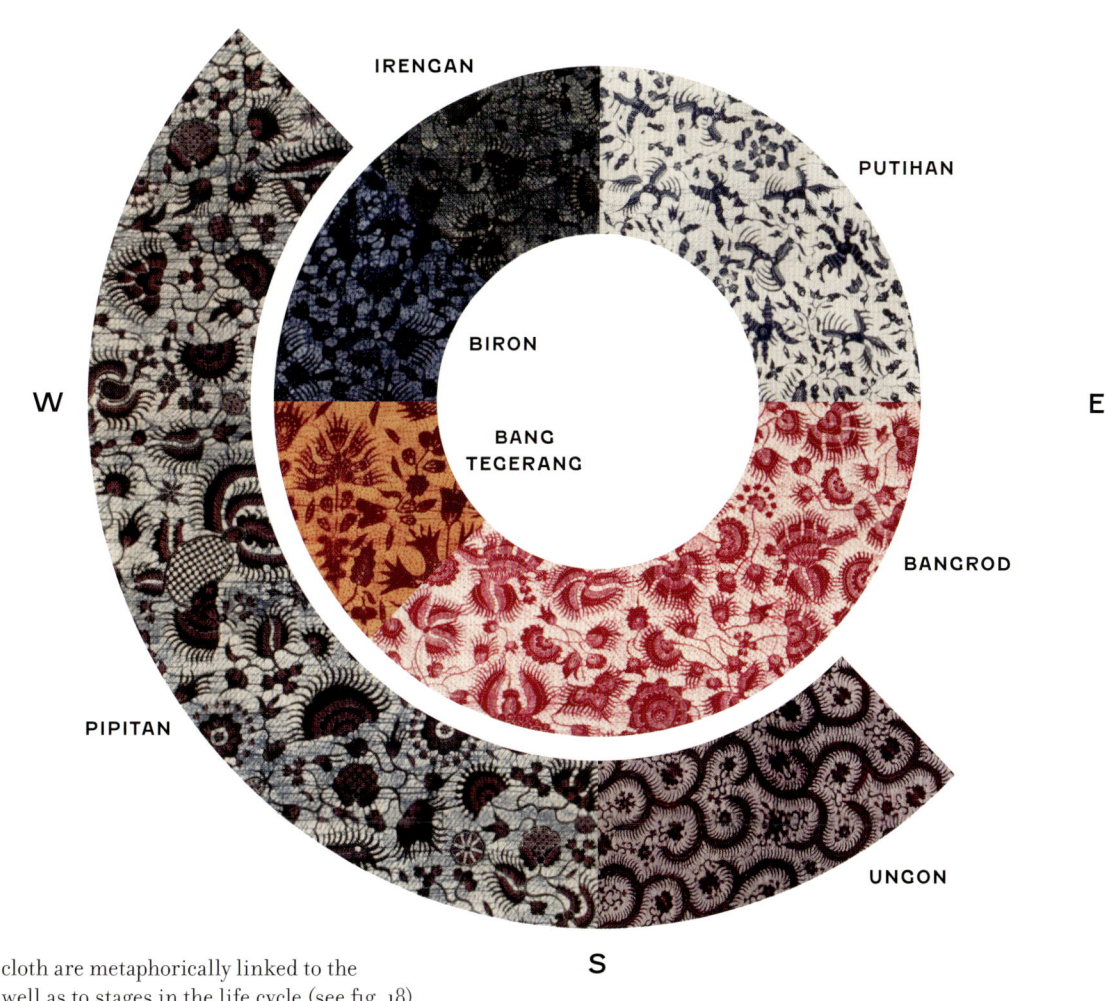

FIGURE 19
Color choices for batik cloth are metaphorically linked to the cardinal directions, as well as to stages in the life cycle (see fig. 18).

The Dress of Individuals

This section presents seventeen sets of dress (pp. 46–79), each reflecting the choices that particular individuals might make based on age, gender, social position, and place of residence. In some cases the messages that a person conveys through dress will work together harmoniously. For example, if a woman is a grandmother, comes from a *sawah*-owning family, and lives in the northern hamlets—all of these factors would indicate the use of dark-colored (*irengan*) batik skirt and shoulder cloths. Figures 20 and 21 show ensembles that work together to consistently convey multiple messages in this way.

In other cases, however, there may be apparent contradictions that need to be reconciled. For example, bright red garments are metaphorically associated with fertility and with the eastern and southern hamlets, yet obviously not all of the women who live in the those hamlets are young and fertile. What is a grandmother from those hamlets to wear? Figures 22 and 23 show ways in which two individuals have responded to contradictions of this nature. In some cases garments may even express relative relationships specific to the contexts of particular events (see fig. 8 for an example).

FIGURE 20
The dark garments reveal that this woman is a resident of the northern hamlets. Even her *pipitan* shoulder cloth is of relatively dark tones compared to similar cloths from other hamlets. Her use of an ikat skirt cloth (*tapeh talenan*) indicates that she belongs to a family of *bakalan*—descendants of the original settled farmers of the northern hamlets. PHOTOGRAPH BY RENS HERINGA, KEREK, 1990.

FIGURE 21
The bright red (*bangrod*) of this woman's shoulder cloth (*sayut*) indicates that she is from the southern hamlets. The brilliant shade, as well as the presence of the *lalat menclat* dotted fringe (see cat. no. 22), signals her status as a fertile young woman. Just visible covering her left knee is her commercial batik skirt cloth (*kain tukon*). This type of cloth is generally worn throughout Kerek by women from landless families or for daily labor. In this case, however, it additionally signals her place of residence in the southern hamlets, whose women are metaphorically considered "new brides" and therefore symbolic "outsiders" (an actual new bride is categorically regarded as an "outsider" throughout Kerek because the patrilocal system requires her to leave her home and live with her husband's family). PHOTOGRAPH BY RENS HERINGA, SIMBATAN (SOUTHERN HAMLETS), KEREK, 1989.

FIGURE 22
Grandmothers are generally expected to dress in dark colors, yet this woman wears a bright red *batik lurik* skirt cloth and a bright red shoulder cloth, not to mention her orange blouse. In this case these garments indicate her area of residence—in the eastern hamlet of Karanglo—rather than her age or reproductive status. The tiny motifs on the shoulder cloth are also characteristic of the eastern hamlets, reflecting the "junior" status of these hamlets compared to the rest of Kerek. Women from the northern or central hamlets would consider this outfit quite garish for an older woman.
PHOTOGRAPH BY RENS HERINGA, KEREK, 1989.

FIGURE 23
Why would this young woman of fertile age wear such dark colors? In this case, her dress reflects her area of residence rather than her age or reproductive status. The dark colors are appropriate for her as a resident of Luwuk, a northern hamlet. PHOTOGRAPH BY RENS HERINGA, KEREK, 1989.

THE DRESS OF INDIVIDUALS

EAST

DRESS FOR A YOUNG KALANG WOMAN OF MARRIAGEABLE AGE

This ensemble consists of two *batik lurik* cloths, befitting a wearer from the Kalang group, the original forest inhabitants of the area. The people of the eastern hamlets are the symbolic "children" of their "elders" in the western hamlets, so eastern patterns are typically tiny in their details. Most *batik lurik* skirts feature dotted patterns on a checked ground as in this skirt, but the shoulder cloth is a rare type that employs floral motifs on a striped ground.

The black and white weft striping (*gelaran,* "like a striped bamboo mat") of the *lurik* ground cloth for the *sayut* is a pattern with protective powers for a person in a liminal position—such as a fertile, unmarried woman. The stippled batik markings on the fringe are called *lalat menclat* (flies hovering close), a thinly veiled sexual metaphor for the droves of suitors hovering nearby (the fringes represent female pubic hair). The pattern name of the skirt cloth, *grompol pacar,* has a double meaning. While the leaves of the *pacar* shrub (henna, *Lawsonia inermis*) are used to paint a bride's nails a brilliant red, a second meaning of *pacar* is "suitor." The bright red color combination, called *bangbangan,* is typical of the eastern hamlets and is also well suited for a bride.

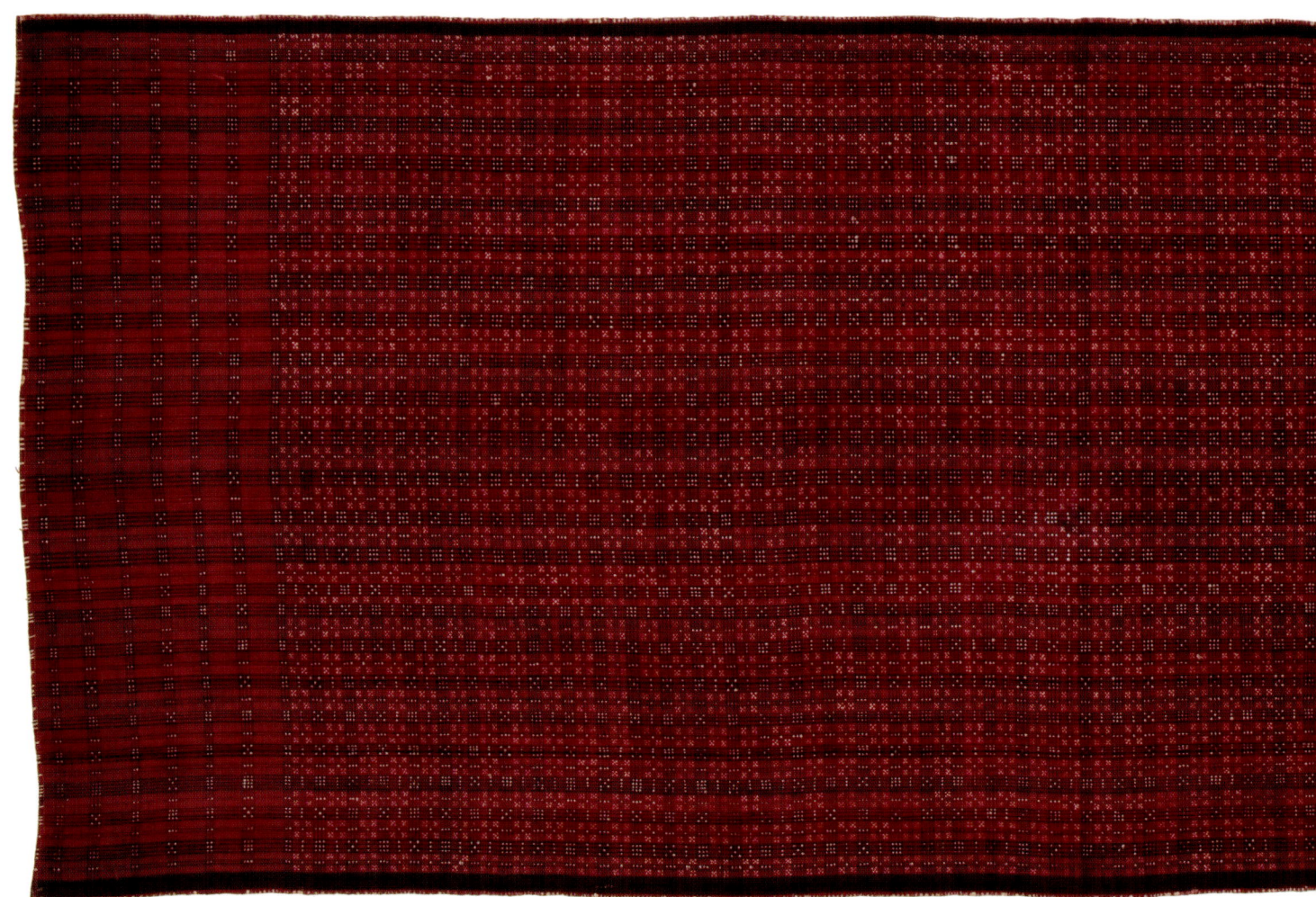

CAT. NO. 21
Woman's skirt cloth (*tapeh*)

Karanglo (eastern hamlets), Kerek, East Java, Indonesia, heirloom when collected in 1989. Batik on handspun/handwoven cotton *lurik*. Pattern name: *grompol pacar* (clusters of suitors). Length 220 cm.
X2008.10.9; PURCHASED BY FOWLER MUSEUM TEXTILE COUNCIL.

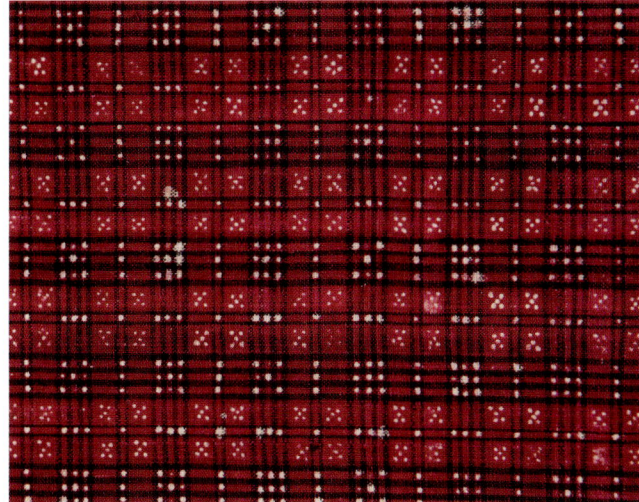

DETAIL OF CAT. NO. 21

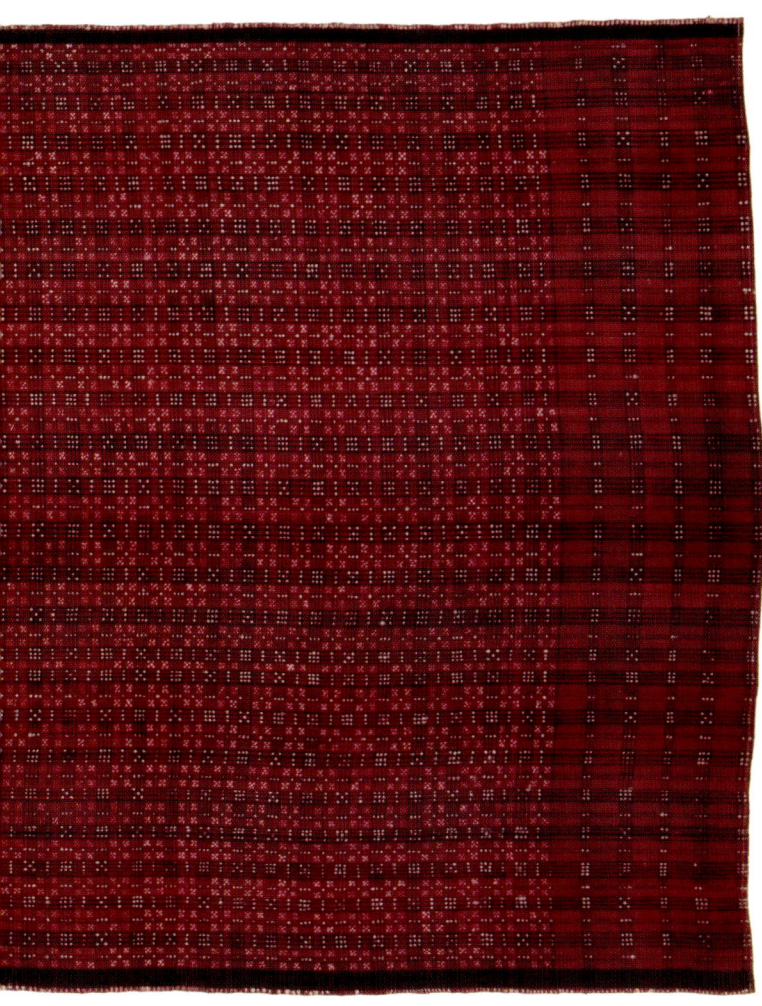

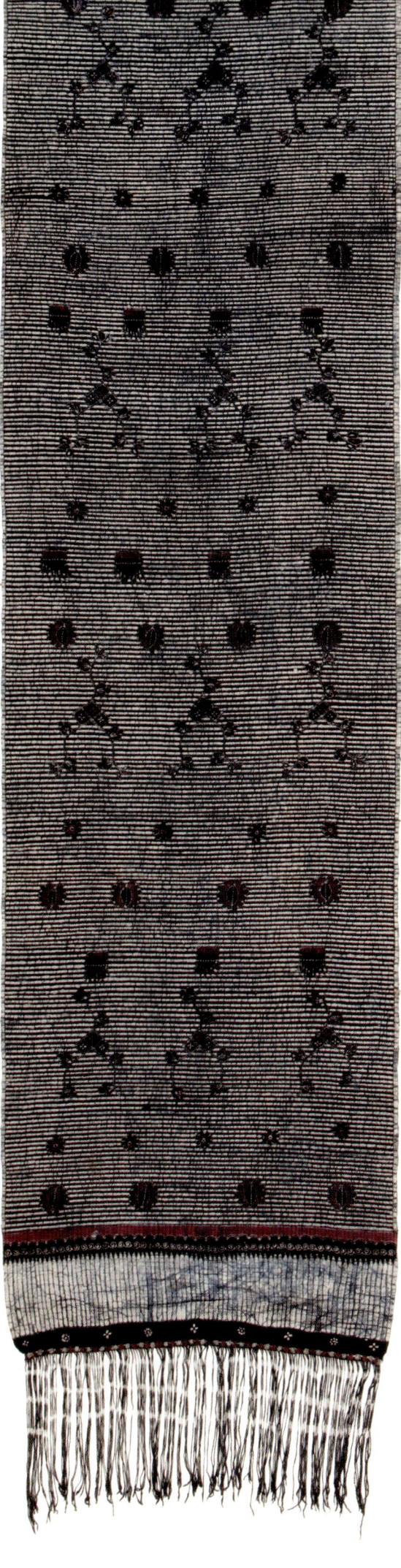

CAT. NO. 22
Woman's shoulder cloth (*sayut*)

Gendong (central hamlets) Kerek, East Java, Indonesia, 1979. Batik on handspun/handwoven cotton *lurik*. Pattern name: *gelaran* (bamboo mat). Width 56 cm. PRIVATE COLLECTION.

EAST

DRESS FOR A RECENT BRIDE, WIFE OF A LANDLESS COMMONER

This shoulder cloth displays a special red-yellow color combination known as *bang tegerang*, which is worn by a bride. Formerly the yellow color was dyed into the ground cloth with scrapings of the root of *Cudrania javanensis* (*tegerang*) before the wax was applied. Today, the cloth is overdyed with yellow synthetic dye after the wax has been removed by boiling. This color and the open central lozenge (*tengahan*) refer to the fertility of a bride.

This cloth was made on a base of natural brown cotton. It was waxed in the eastern hamlet of Karanglo, an area of relatively low status that was not traditionally regarded as a center for the production of fine batik. In the last decade, however, the women of Karanglo have become active producers and are now making quality batik featuring their own eastern patterns. The pattern name *laseman* indicates a style associated with Lasem, a famous center for North Coast batik.

The pattern of the *lurik* skirt cloth, *ksatriyan*, takes its name from the traditional Hindu warrior caste of ancient Java. This is an example of a *lurik* pattern reflecting a specific occupation, as it used to serve as the uniform of conscripted villagers serving the ruler of Tuban in times of war. In earlier times, wives would follow their husbands to war. Today only women continue to wear the dress that reflects their husbands' erstwhile status or occupation. The relatively bright shades of both the red and blue colors are appropriate for the eastern hamlets.

CAT. NO. 23
Woman's shoulder cloth (*sayut*)

Karanglo (eastern hamlets), Kerek, East Java, Indonesia, 2004. Batik on handspun/handwoven natural brown cotton (*lawon lawa*). Color combination: *bang tegerang*. Pattern name: *laseman*, with central lozenge (*tengahan*). Width 65 cm. PRIVATE COLLECTION.

DETAIL OF CAT. NO. 24

CAT. NO. 24
Woman's tube skirt (*sarung*)

Karanglo (eastern hamlets), Kerek, East Java, Indonesia, heirloom when collected in 1989. Handspun/handwoven cotton (*lurik*). Pattern name: *ksatriyan*. Length 92 cm. X2008.10.3; PURCHASED BY FOWLER MUSEUM TEXTILE COUNCIL.

THE DRESS OF INDIVIDUALS 49

SOUTHEAST

DRESS FOR AN ELITE MOTHER, WIFE OF AN OWNER OF *SAWAH* LANDS

The origin stories of the southeastern hamlets, located at the hazardous point where a "child" is about to turn into a "mature woman," bewail the fate of an abandoned bride. Reputedly this lot befalls many women of these hamlets. Forced to fend for themselves, they become bridal dressers or singers and dancers performing at weddings.

Only members of the elite, the owners of the most favored wet rice agricultural lands (*sawah*), dress completely in locally made batik for both top and bottom garments. The *pipitan* color combination of the shoulder cloth marks the wearer as a mother in the middle of the life cycle. Its motifs are associated with fertility: the sun, the moon, and birds carrying rice stalks. The flowers and birds are slightly larger than those of the east, while the hues are relatively bright, appropriate for the southeastern region.

The skirt cloth is extra long, indicating that it is an heirloom cloth. It features an unusual color combination known as *ungon* (purple) that belongs to the southeast. One might expect a cloth of this color to belong more with the dark colors of the north, but to Javanese eyes red and blue dyes of the same medium strength combine into a purple color, complementing each other as a bridal couple do. Newly opened flowers grow from the smallish roundels of the waterweed (*ganggeng*) trailing over the field.

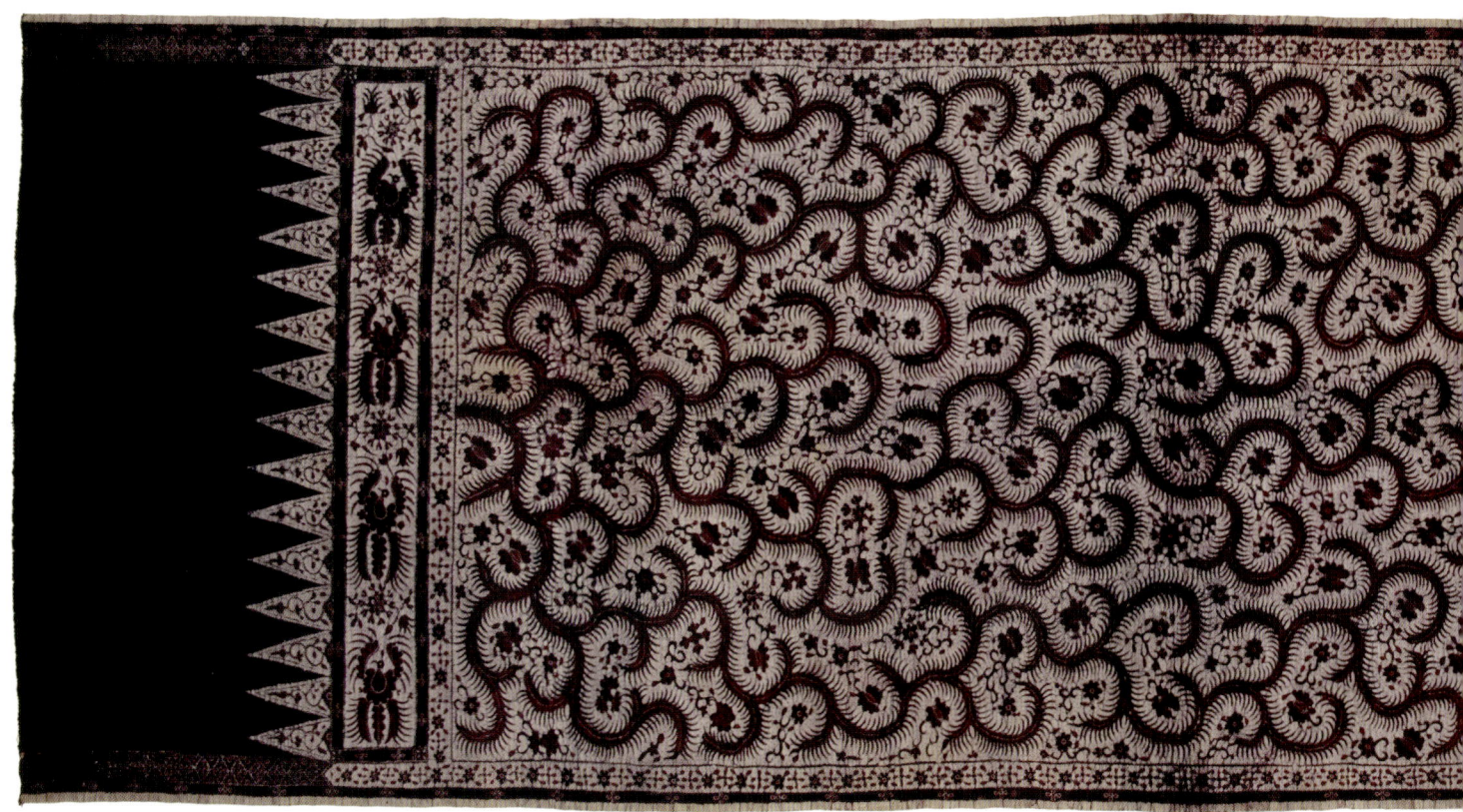

CAT. NO. 25
Woman's skirt cloth (*jarit*)

Temayang (southeastern hamlets), Kerek, East Java, Indonesia, heirloom when collected in 1996. Batik on handspun/handwoven cotton. Color combination: *ungon*. Pattern name: *ganggeng* (water weed). Length 239 cm. X2008.10.20; PURCHASED BY FOWLER MUSEUM TEXTILE COUNCIL.

CAT. NO. 26

Shoulder cloth (*sayut*)

Temayang (southeastern hamlets), Kerek, East Java, Indonesia, heirloom when collected in 1980. Batik on handspun/handwoven cotton. Color combination: *pipitan*. Pattern name: *laseman*. Width 56 cm. X2008.10.14; PURCHASED BY FOWLER MUSEUM TEXTILE COUNCIL.

THE DRESS OF INDIVIDUALS 51

SOUTH

DRESS FOR A NUBILE YOUNG WOMAN OF MARRIAGEABLE AGE

The brightest garments in all of Kerek announce that a young woman is on the verge of becoming a full, married member of the community. She will combine a bright red Kerek shoulder cloth with an even more eye-catching skirt cloth purchased in the local market.

Kerek's southern hamlets are known for the brightest red shoulder cloths. If a cloth of high quality is desired, however, it will often be ordered from batik makers in the central hamlets. This shoulder cloth was waxed by the daughter in the only remaining family of hereditary dyers, a gifted artist. She used the characteristic fertility-inducing motifs of the south rather than those of her own hamlet. The motifs include the sun and the moon; lotus blossoms (*kembang teratai*), which are symbolically related to marital bliss; and swallows (*manuk sikatan*), which always fly in pairs.

For market-bought skirt cloths, Kerek women usually favor the products of one of the professional batik makers in Prunggahan, the onetime seat of the first *patih* (ruler) of Tuban (see p. 84). Because they have to be purchased with scarce cash income, the base cloth is usually of relatively low quality. In this cloth, the three zigzag bands covering the field in contrasting shades show three different phases of life in nature: *ungkeran* (resembling the cocoons of a butterfly), *ukel* (newly grown tender sprouts), and *kedele kecer* ("scattered soybeans," or the seeds for next year's growing cycle).

CAT. NO. 27
Woman's commercial batik skirt cloth (*kain tukon*)

Prunggahan, Tuban, East Java, Indonesia, late 1970s. Batik on machine-woven cotton. Pattern name: *keteguk dengkul* (bent knees). Length 240 cm. PRIVATE COLLECTION.

CAT. NO. 28
Woman's shoulder cloth (*sayut*)

Gendong (central hamlets), Kerek, East Java, Indonesia, late 1970s. Batik on handspun/handwoven cotton. Color combination: *bangrod*. Pattern name: *laseman*. Width 59 cm. X2008.10.12; PURCHASED BY FOWLER MUSEUM TEXTILE COUNCIL.

SOUTHWEST

DRESS FOR A BRIDE OF THE *TEGAL*-OWNING CLASS

For the *salinan* ceremony, a ritual change of clothing at the conclusion of a Javanese wedding, the bride and groom put on garments befitting their newly married status and then sit in state on a dais before the assembled community. In Kerek, they are said to embody the rice goddess, Mbok Sri, and her consort, Jaka Sedana, and this ceremony marks the bride's newly acquired membership in her husband's family

The yellow and red shoulder cloth is an example of the special color combination for a bride, which is called *bang tegerang*. The rather muted red is typical of the western half of Kerek. The cloth's relatively large-sized flowers are fully opened while the grown birds spread their wings to fly away, like the bride who will move to her husband's house.

Yellow also appears in the supplementary-weft yarns of the bride's skirt cloth, in the form of market-bought mercerized cotton yarn (*benang bola kuning*) woven into a naturally dyed, muted red morinda (*mengkudu*) base. The teak blossoms in the pattern refer to the fragrant, flowering teak trees at the beginning of the rainy season and also to the ancestors—small stands of teak trees near graveyards are all that remain of the dense forests that once covered the area. The supplementary-weft patterning gives the cloth a brighter appearance on one side than the other. A young bride wears the bright side out; the darker side would be appropriate in later life.

CAT. NO. 29
Woman's shoulder cloth (*sayut*)

Tengger Wetan (southwestern hamlets), Kerek, East Java, Indonesia, heirloom when collected in 1984. Batik on handspun/handwoven cotton. Color combination: *bang tegerang*. Pattern name: *laseman*. Width 58 cm.
X2008.10.13; PURCHASED BY FOWLER MUSEUM TEXTILE COUNCIL.

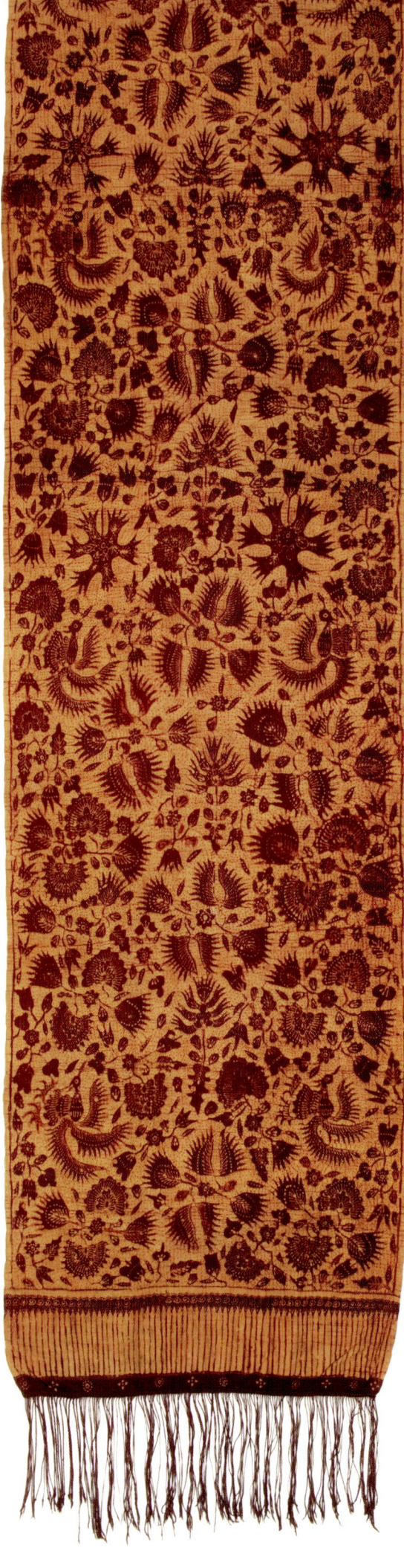

CAT. NO. 30
Woman's skirt cloth (*tapeh*)

Probably Ngaji (western hamlets), Kerek, East Java, Indonesia, early twentieth century. Handspun/handwoven cotton with supplementary weft (*lurik kembangan*). Pattern name: *kembang jati* (teak blossom). Length 271 cm. X2008.10.7; PURCHASED BY FOWLER MUSEUM TEXTILE COUNCIL.

DETAIL OF CAT. NO. 30

SOUTHWEST

DRESS FOR A BRIDEGROOM OF THE *TEGAL*-OWNING CLASS

The wedding jacket is given the title *kelambi rasukan* in Javanese, a poetic, honorific, and redundant usage (both *kelambi* and *rasukan* mean "jacket," one in high-register formal Javanese and the other in low-register). This jacket features an old warp-float pattern that is no longer made, with shop-bought cotton yarn. It was purchased from the cloth dealer in Ngaji and was probably made there as well, as this western hamlet specializes in high-quality pattern weaves.

The groom's pants, batiked especially for this purpose, are referred to as *celana gringsing*. The Old Javanese term *gringsing* (against illness) refers to the protective function of the garment. A twelfth-century Javanese epic relates that *gringsing* pants of this style—though not necessarily batik—were presented by the ruler to his warriors before he sent them into combat. For a man to embark upon marriage is also considered a phase of life fraught with danger. The pattern *kembang manggar* (areca blossom) shows flowering stalks of the areca palm with their tiny knob-like buds unopened. As floral arrangements set beside the bridal pair, these countless tiny and heavily fragrant buds express a hope for many offspring.

Neither of these garments would have been made in the southwestern hamlets, and they might be used anywhere in the western part of Kerek by descendants of *tegal* owners. Symbolically, however, they are regarded as belonging to the southwest due to the place of the newly wedded couple in the cycle of life.

CAT. NO. 31
Man's jacket (*kelambi rasukan*)

Ngaji (western hamlets), Kerek, East Java, Indonesia, heirloom when collected in 1980. Handspun/handwoven cotton with warp-float patterning. Pattern name: *bolong buntu potong inten* (clogged hole, cut through with a diamond). Length 67 cm. PRIVATE COLLECTION.

CAT. NO. 32
Man's pants (*celana gringsing*)

Gendong (central hamlets), pre-1940. Batik on handspun/handwoven cotton. Color combination: *irengan*. Pattern name: *kembang manggar*. Length 98 cm. PRIVATE COLLECTION.

WEDDING CANOPY

A wedding canopy (*lelangit*, "firmament-like") shields the couple as they sit in state following the wedding. Cloths used as *lelangit* often follow the *buntungan* design format (see p. 19). When worn as skirts, *buntungan* cloths are appropriate for post-menopausal women rather than brides, but as a wedding canopy, the *buntungan* cloth signals the approval of the ancestors.

This *lelangit* is waxed mostly in archaic dotted lines. Its color combination—medium blue with white patterns—is the opposite of a floral *biron* cloth, but, nonetheless, it is called *biron* as well and has the same protective properties. The abstracted pattern bears the fitting name *rengganis*, an angel in the Muslim *swarga*, the heavenly paradise.

CAT. NO. 33
Wedding canopy (*lelangit*)

Gendong (central hamlets), Kerek, East Java, Indonesia, heirloom when collected pre-1940. Batik on handspun/handwoven cotton. Color combination: *biron*. Pattern name: *rengganis* (name of an Islamic angel). Length 298 cm. PRIVATE COLLECTION.

WEST

DRESS FOR A KALANG MOTHER OF MIDDLE AGE

The shoulder cloth with the *pipitan* color combination marks the wearer as a mother of middle age, while the *batik lurik* skirt cloth identifies her as a member of the Kalang (the original forest-dwelling inhabitants of the area). The shoulder cloth can be presumed to have been made in Ngaji (western hamlets) based on the large motifs and also on the rather muted red and blue colors, which are not as bright as they would be on a similar cloth from the east or south. Among the motifs are pairs of swallows (*manuk sikatan*), which are considered appropriate for married women.

The muted red skirt cloth is made in the *sisihan* design format, with different patterns at each end of the cloth. The two densely dotted patterns require a special base fabric, referred to as *baju butha* (demon's dress), which is characterized by small black and white checks. The diagonal pattern on the right is *kejing miring* (fallen tombstones), a reference to the extended genealogies of the Kalang found in fourteenth-century land acts. The left side shows the *batik lurik* version of the checked *ksatriyan* pattern (compare cat. no. 24), indicating that Kalang also followed in the train of the army of the ruler of Tuban, carrying supplies in their ox carts. The wearer can adjust her cloth to show either pattern depending upon the occasion.

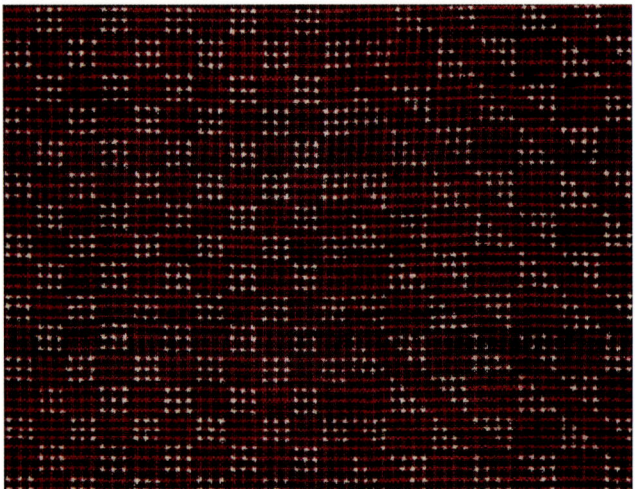

CAT. NO. 34
Woman's skirt cloth with two patterns (*tapeh sisihan*)

Ngaji (western hamlets), Kerek, East Java, Indonesia, 1989. Batik on handspun/handwoven checked cotton cloth (*lurik*). Pattern names: *kejing miring* and *ksatriyan*. Color type: *bangbangan*. Length 258 cm. X2008.10.8; PURCHASED BY FOWLER MUSEUM TEXTILE COUNCIL.

DETAIL OF CAT. NO. 34

CAT. NO. 35

Woman's shoulder cloth (*sayut*)

Ngaji (western hamlets), Kerek, East Java, Indonesia, 1979. Batik on handspun/handwoven checked cotton cloth (*lurik*). Color combination: *pipitan*. Pattern name: *laseman*. Width 58 cm. X2008.26.23; GIFT OF MARY JANE LELAND.

THE DRESS OF INDIVIDUALS 59

CAT. NO. 36
Woman's tubular skirt (*sarung*)

Ngaji (western hamlets), Kerek, East Java, Indonesia, 1950s.
Handspun/handwoven cotton. Pattern name: *ksatriyan*.
Length 82 cm. X2008.26.21; GIFT OF MARY JANE LELAND.

WEST

DRESS FOR A MOTHER OF MIDDLE AGE, WIFE OF A LANDLESS COMMONER

The *lurik* skirt is appropriate for the wife of a man who owned no land himself but worked the land of others. The pattern *ksatriyan* indicates that his ancestors were among the followers of the *patih*, or ruler, of Tuban in times of war. The seemingly complicated, basketweave pattern of the skirt cloth is merely the result of a special warping technique. The skirt cloth can be dated to the 1950s by the fading of what was once the red color. At that time, the high-quality natural dyes for red had already gone out of use, but modern colorfast synthetic dyes had not yet been introduced. Only poor-quality chemical dyes were available to weavers during that period.

The pattern on the batik shoulder cloth is typical of the west, as it has neither the finely detailed motifs of the east and south nor the dense filler motifs of the center. An interesting detail is a broody hen (*babon anggrem*) sitting on her nest. Women from the other hamlets consider the style of the cloth rather brash and vulgar, attributes popularly associated with the people from the west themselves. The long fringes are elaborately knotted at their bases (*krawangan*).

CAT. NO. 37
Woman's shoulder cloth (*sayut*)

Tengger Wetan (southwestern hamlets), Kerek, East Java, Indonesia, acquired in 1984. Batik on handspun/handwoven cotton. Color combination: *bangrod*. Pattern name: *laseman*. Width 59 cm.
PRIVATE COLLECTION.

DETAIL OF CAT. NO. 36

THE DRESS OF INDIVIDUALS

NORTHWEST

DRESS FOR AN ELITE GRANDMOTHER, WIFE OF THE OWNER OF *SAWAH* LANDS

Flower and bird motifs are usually executed separately, but the motifs on this shoulder cloth show how they are sometimes fused in the northern hamlets. The first row features a floral form combined with the bird *manuk jimprak*, the male of which is known for hopping up and down (*jimprak*) while courting the female. In the second row the floral forms are combined with *manuk gemek*, the female quail that is used in Java as a fighting bird. The motif shows the bird in full attack. These bird motifs appear in rows of three, a metaphor for the three generations of descendants over which a grandmother presides (her own, that of her daughter, and that of her granddaughter).

The skirt cloth is a rare example of a Kerek batik made on imported rather than locally woven cotton cloth. Called *kain makau* after the southern Chinese port of Macau, which was once its source, this cloth ceased to be imported to Java early in the twentieth century. The pattern is closely related to another common pattern, *ganggeng* (waterweed). Here the winding forms are given another meaning, as representations of poisonous centipedes (*kelabang*) wandering (*melaku*) over the surface of the cloth. This is particularly appropriate for a blue and white cloth, which has protective functions, as the centipedes are seen as offering additional protection for the wearer. A seam, faintly visible in the center of the cloth, marks the place where a tuck has been taken to repair a worn section. Such repairs are nearly always found in the part of the cloth that is worn at the back, as that area wears out first.

CAT. NO. 38
Woman's skirt cloth (*jarit*)

Gendong (central hamlets) Kerek, East Java, Indonesia, early twentieth century. Batik on imported cotton cloth. Color combination: *biron*. Pattern name: *kelabang melaku* (wandering centipede). Length 229 cm. PRIVATE COLLECTION.

CAT. NO. 39
Woman's shoulder cloth (*sayut*)

Gendong (central hamlets), Kerek, East Java, Indonesia, heirloom when collected in 1979. Batik on handspun/handwoven cotton. Color combination: *irengan*. Pattern name: *kenanga ginubah* (transformed *kenanga* blossom). Width 56 cm. X2008.10.15; PURCHASED BY FOWLER MUSEUM TEXTILE COUNCIL.

NORTHWEST

DRESS FOR AN ELITE GRANDFATHER, OWNER OF *SAWAH* LANDS

The *lurik talenan* fabric is intended for making a man's tailored jacket (*kelambi*). Characteristically, ikat fabric for men carries the pattern in the warp only, whereas ikat for women has patterning in both warp and weft. Only a man of the elite *sawah*-owning group would wear an *irengan* batik cloth on the lower body for official occasions. The man's tube skirt (*sarung amba*) is longer than a woman's. Since a weaver's arm span is not long enough to allow her to make a sufficiently wide single panel of cloth for a *sarung amba*, the skirt is constructed from two panels of cloth. Men's high-status *sarung amba* always show abstract white motifs on an indigo-dyed, deep blue-black ground. The pattern *kelapa sekantet* (coconuts clustered on the same tree) is a male genealogical reference.

CAT. NO. 40

Detail of fabric for a man's jacket (*bakal kelambi*)

Ngaji (western hamlets), Kerek, East Java, Indonesia, 1979. Handspun/handwoven cotton with ikat in the warp. Pattern name: *lanjar sisig* (young widow with blackened teeth). X2008.10.4; PURCHASED BY FOWLER MUSEUM TEXTILE COUNCIL.

CAT. NO. 41A,B
Two panels of fabric for a man's tubular skirt cloth (*sarung amba*)

Gendong (central hamlets), Kerek, East Java, Indonesia, heirloom when collected in 1981. Batik on handspun/handwoven cotton. Color combination: *irengan*. Pattern name: *kelapa sekantet* (coconuts clustered on the same tree). Length 155 cm. PRIVATE COLLECTION.

NORTH

DRESS FOR A KALANG GRANDMOTHER

These cloths are appropriate for women of advanced age and also for those from the north. The black-and-white weft-striped shoulder cloth with unfinished short fringes represents one of the earliest types of cloth and is considered the one with the ultimate protective potential. A legendary woman once survived the threat of drowning in a sudden flood because she wore this pattern, known as *tuwuh watu* ("rock-bodied," or immortal).

The *batik lurik* skirt cloth has the extra length that marks an heirloom cloth. Cloths made for ordinary purposes are at least one hand span shorter. The cloth was dyed with indigo and then over-dyed with *sogo tingi*, a type of mangrove bark, to darken it further. The tiny triangles along the border (*untu walang*, "crickets' teeth") are an added protective touch.

CAT. NO. 42
Woman's shoulder cloth (*sayut*)

Ngaji (western hamlets), Kerek, East Java, Indonesia, 1984. Hand-spun/handwoven cotton. Pattern name: *tuwuh watu* (rock bodied). Width 59 cm. PRIVATE COLLECTION.

DETAIL OF CAT. NO. 43

CAT. NO. 43
Woman's skirt cloth (*tapeh*)

Luwuk (northern hamlets), Kerek, East Java, Indonesia, heirloom when collected in 1989. Batik on handspun/handwoven checked cloth (*lurik*). Color combination: *irengan*. Pattern: *cuken* (like a quilted mattress). Length 270 cm. X2008.10.10; PURCHASED BY FOWLER MUSEUM TEXTILE COUNCIL.

THE DRESS OF INDIVIDUALS 67

NORTH

FUNERAL SHROUD

This type of shroud is used by all social groups in Kerek. The dark color, associated with death and the north, stems from a final dye bath in mud, which is considered analogous to the "planting" of the body in the grave. The cloth will serve to cover the deceased while a ritual bath is prepared. Laid out in the central area of the house, the corpse is secluded behind four heirloom skirt cloths made with different techniques and colors, representing the male ancestors of the deceased. After the purification ritual, the corpse is wrapped in a white Muslim *kain kafan*, prayed over, and laid on the bier. Sheltered by the same four cloths and then tied across with three *sayut* (*bangrod*, *pipitan*, and *irengan*), the deceased will be carried to the graveyard. All of the covering cloths will be taken home after the funeral and washed by the grandchildren to be saved as heirlooms (*pusaka* or *simpenan*) or used as part of the bridal gift. In this way, cloths may acquire a pedigree that women remember.

CAT. NO. 44
Funeral shroud

Kerek, East Java, Indonesia, heirloom when collected in 1990. Batik on handspun/handwoven *lurik* cloth. Color: *irengan*. Pattern name: unknown. Length 253 cm. PRIVATE COLLECTION.

FIGURE 24
A funeral bier, covered with heirloom skirt cloths, is additionally wrapped with three *sayut* of different colors. PHOTOGRAPH BY RENS HERINGA, LUWUK (NORTHERN HAMLETS), KEREK, 1990.

DETAIL OF CAT. NO. 44

NORTH

DRESS FOR A YOUNG GIRL OF AN ELITE *SAWAH*-OWNING FAMILY

If north is the direction of old age and death, these stages in the life cycle are also seen as necessary precursors to regeneration. By the time a woman reaches old age, she is ideally surrounded by generations of descendants.

This tiny *sarung* was made for a girl in the northern hamlet of Luwuk and presented to her at the age of five, when she ceremonially donned her first skirt cloth. Her father's eldest brother's wife made the motifs smaller than normal to keep them in proportion with the size of the garment. The style of the cloth is not entirely typical of Kerek, as the maker came from Bongkol, a batik-making hamlet closer to Tuban (see p. 84). It is common for high-class women to marry outside their home area as they are supposed to marry "up" in status and often cannot find appropriate partners locally.

CAT. NO. 45
Girl's first tube skirt (*sarung anak*)

Luwuk (northern hamlets), Kerek, East Java, Indonesia, circa 1970. Batik on handspun/handwoven cotton. Color combination: *bangrod*. Pattern name: *cluken* (resembling a carnation). Length 53 cm.
X2008.10.26; PURCHASED BY FOWLER MUSEUM TEXTILE COUNCIL.

THE DRESS OF INDIVIDUALS

CENTER

DRESS FOR A DYER

Women in all of Kerek's hamlets wax their own batik patterns, but the central hamlets are where the finest batiks are normally made. Women there must know the patterns from all of the hamlets so that they can make pieces ordered from them. Moreover, all of the dyeing is done in the center. Today there is only a single family in Gendong (central hamlets) that does most of the dyeing for Kerek. In the past, there were dyers in one other central hamlet, Kajoran.

Indigo dyeing is regarded as a ritual activity, and when the dyer is engaged in this process, she wears an archaic form of dress consisting of an inexpensive commercial batik worn as an undercloth, over which is wrapped a locally produced batik. The local cloth is wrapped high over the breasts, in a style known as *kembenan* ("like a *kemben*," referring to an older style of long breast-wrap cloth that is still used today in Bali, whereas the breast cloths used in Central Java are much shorter). The strong blue *biron* color combination of this cloth is thought to encourage successful results in the dyeing.

CAT. NO. 46

Woman's overcloth (*jarit*)

Kajoran (central hamlets), Kerek, East Java, Indonesia, heirloom when collected in 1979. Batik on handspun/handwoven cotton. Color combination: *biron*. Pattern name: *melati selangsang* (a banana-leaf cone full of jasmine flowers, sold in the market for use in ceremonies). Length 266 cm. X2008.10.25; PURCHASED BY FOWLER MUSEUM TEXTILE COUNCIL.

CAT. NO. 47
Woman's commercial batik skirt cloth (*kain tukon*)

Palang, Tuban Regency, East Java, Indonesia, 1990s. Batik on industrially woven cotton cloth. Pattern name: *gringsing tempel lunglungan* (dragon scales with floral overlay; see also p. 57). Length 242 cm. PRIVATE COLLECTION.

DETAIL OF CAT. NO. 46

THE DRESS OF INDIVIDUALS

CENTER

DRESS FOR A MIDWIFE

Many weaving areas around the world once maintained varieties of cotton that produced tan or light brown fibers rather than white, but these have gradually fallen out of favor. Kerek is one of the few places where sacred brown cotton, called *kapas lawa* (fruit bat's cotton) in Javanese, is still grown. It is farmed in separate fields from white cotton and is regarded as the prerogative of the village midwife's lineage. Symbolically, the brown cotton is associated with regeneration and is thus particularly appropriate for the garments of a midwife.

The brown cotton that was used for this shoulder cloth was owned by the midwife, given to a weaver to make up into cloth, then given to a batik specialist in the central hamlets (for waxing), and finally taken to the dyer. The color combination is *pipitan*, but the tan color of the cotton gives the cloth a different appearance. The midwife is easily recognized in her professional capacity when wearing this shoulder cloth on her way to visit a client.

When at work inside the house, delivering a baby or tending to the mother, the midwife wears a type of camisole (*kutang*), which she covers with a blouse (*kebaya*) when leaving the compound. The white and bright blue *lurik* fabric illustrated here is intended for making this *kutang*. The ritual name for the pattern, *intip hiyan*, refers to the plaited bamboo tray on which newly steamed rice is spread and fanned in order to make the steam rise up as an offering to the ancestors.

CAT. NO. 48
Detail of fabric for a camisole (*bakal kutang*)

Gendong (central hamlets), Kerek, East Java, Indonesia, 1983. Handspun/handwoven cotton. Pattern name: *intip hiyan* (ritual bamboo tray) or *gedekan* (like plaited bamboo). X2008.10.2; PURCHASED BY FOWLER MUSEUM TEXTILE COUNCIL.

CAT. NO. 49
Woman's shoulder cloth (*sayut*)

Gendong (central hamlets), Kerek, East Java, Indonesia, 1989. Batik on handspun/handwoven natural brown cotton. Color combination: *pipitan*. Pattern name: *laseman*. Width 59 cm. X2008.10.17; PURCHASED BY FOWLER MUSEUM TEXTILE COUNCIL.

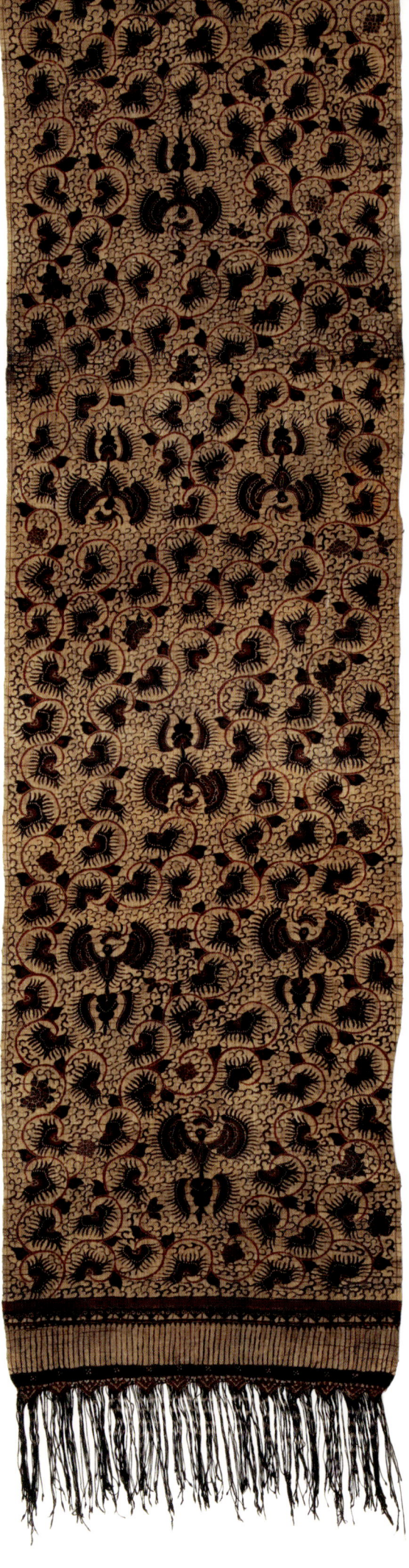

CAT. NO. 50
Woman's tube skirt (*sarung*)

Ngaji (western hamlets), Kerek, East Java, Indonesia, 1979. Handspun/handwoven cotton with compound ikat. Pattern name: *dom semelap* (needle and thread passing through a cloth). Length 95 cm.
X2008.10.5; PURCHASED BY FOWLER MUSEUM TEXTILE COUNCIL.

DETAIL OF CAT. NO. 46

THE DRESS OF INDIVIDUALS   73

CENTER

DRESS FOR THE WIFE OF THE *KEBAYAN*

A *kebayan* is the spokesman who mediates between the village chief and the populace. When the chief needs to inform the people of the village of any kind of emergency, such as a death or a fire, he orders the *kebayan* to sound the appropriate signal on the *kentongan*, a hollow wooden or bamboo signal block that hangs outside the chief's house. The chief and the *kebayan* of the central hamlets formerly acted as mediators between all the hamlets of Kerek and the authorities in Tuban. Today this task has been taken over by officials in the government's district (*kecamatan*) office.

Skirt cloths with relatively large abstract motifs on a blue-black ground are worn by prominent senior women whose husbands have a special standing in the community. This particular heirloom cloth was formerly in the possession of the retired *kebayan*'s wife, a person of high status in her own right as the owner of the main house in her large family compound. In keeping with her social position, the skirt features the abstracted blossoms of the giant kapok tree (*randu*, *Ceiba pentandra*), which towers up to 200 feet over its surroundings. The tree gives shelter to many kinds of plants and animals, among them the fruit bats that spread its seeds after being attracted by the smell of its white flowers.

The finely drawn, fluttering birds on the shoulder cloth also accord well with the image of this tree. The fringe has been cut off this cloth indicating that it has been used in some ritual context.

CAT. NO. 51
Woman's skirt cloth (*jarit*)

Gendong (central hamlets), Kerek, East Java, Indonesia, heirloom when collected in 1979. Batik on handspun/handwoven cotton. Color combination: *irengan*. Pattern name: *kembang randu* (kapok blossom). Length 294 cm. X2008.10.24; PURCHASED BY FOWLER MUSEUM TEXTILE COUNCIL.

CAT. NO. 52
Woman's shoulder cloth (*sayut*)

Gendong (central hamlets), Kerek, East Java, Indonesia, heirloom when collected in 1979. Batik on handspun/handwoven cotton. Color combination: *putihan*. Pattern name: *manuk mibir* (fluttering birds). Width 56 cm. PRIVATE COLLECTION.

THE DRESS OF INDIVIDUALS 75

CENTER

DRESS FOR THE VILLAGE CHIEF

Just as a brown cotton garment is used by the midwife due to its association with regeneration, brown cotton is used in the pants and jacket worn by the village chief at the time of the ceremonial rice planting and the harvest. Slung across his chest, he wears a bright red tube skirt (*sarung amba*)—the same color that is worn by the fertile young bride-to-be. (See fig. 5.)

On close examination, the sturdy fabric of the pants and jacket, called *usik lawa*, can be seen to have a finely stippled appearance. This results from the use of a two-ply weft yarn made with one strand of white cotton and one strand of brown. The fabric was ordered from an accomplished weaver, the late Mbok Tarmini, in the western hamlets.

CAT. NO. 53A,B
Pants (*celana kagok*) and jacket (*kelambi*)

Ngaji (western hamlets), Kerek, East Java, Indonesia, 1984. Hand-spun/handwoven brown and white cotton. Length of pants 82 cm.
X2008.10.1A,B; PURCHASED BY FOWLER MUSEUM TEXTILE COUNCIL.

CAT. NO. 54
Man's tube skirt (*sarung amba*)

Gendong (central hamlets), Kerek, East Java, Indonesia, heirloom when collected in 1978. Batik on handspun/handwoven cotton. Color combination: *bangrod*. Pattern name: *cluken* (resembling a carnation). Length 108 cm. X2008.10.18; PURCHASED BY FOWLER MUSEUM TEXTILE COUNCIL.

CENTER

DRESS FOR THE VILLAGE CHIEF'S WIFE

The elements of the pattern in this shoulder cloth hint at the role of the Chinese in bringing Islam to the north coast of Java. The background pattern, named *owal-awil* (locally pronounced *wal-awil*), is related to the Chinese *banji* (ten thousand) motif, which is regarded as protective and also appears on carved wooden door frames. One of the round motifs, the *manuk huk*, represents "the bird bringing *hok*" ("*hok*" being Chinese for "good fortune"), which is a symbol of the coming of Islam to Java. It depicts an egg that fell from the sky, and in it a bird with a message in its beak, the Islamic Profession of Faith. The other round motif is *piring aji*, representing a priceless imported Chinese ceramic plate, also regarded as having magical protective powers.

The skirt cloth was made in 1989 following the pattern of an heirloom skirt owned by the village chief's wife.

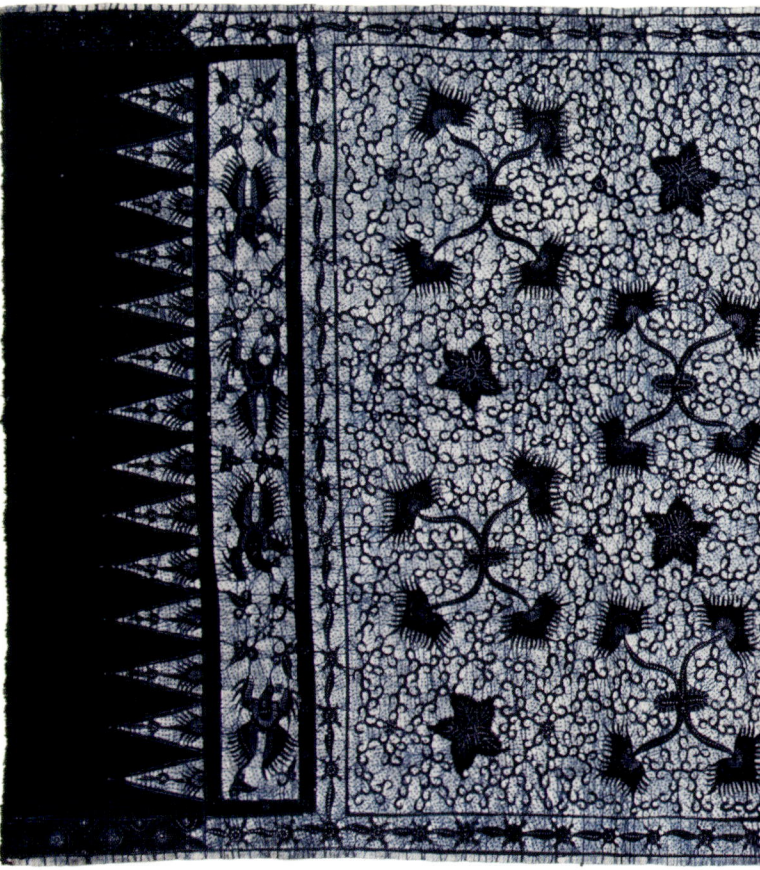

CAT. NO. 55

Woman's shoulder cloth (*sayut*)

Gendong (central hamlets), Kerek, East Java, Indonesia, heirloom when collected in 1984. Batik on handspun/handwoven cotton. Color combination: *biron*. Pattern name: *owal-awil* (scattered in all directions). Width 57 cm. X2008.10.23; PURCHASED BY FOWLER MUSEUM TEXTILE COUNCIL.

DETAIL OF CAT. NO. 56

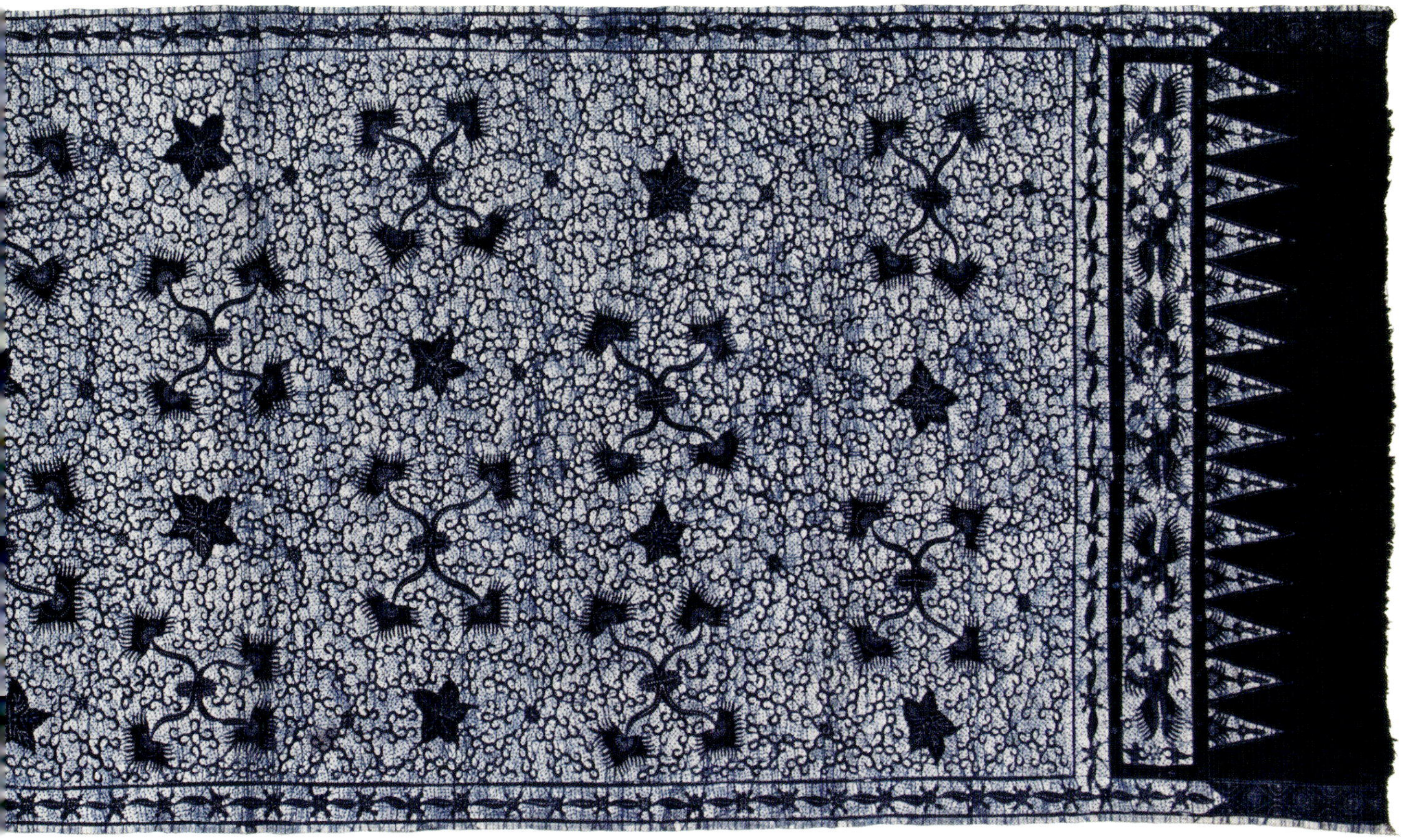

CAT. NO. 56
Woman's skirt cloth (*jarit*)

Gendong (central hamlets), Kerek, East Java, Indonesia, 1989. Batik on handspun/handwoven cotton. Color combination: *putihan*. Pattern name: *dampyang pokal* (clustered sprouts of a banana tree). Length 254 cm. X2008.10.22; PURCHASED BY FOWLER MUSEUM TEXTILE COUNCIL.

THE DRESS OF INDIVIDUALS   79

Recent Changes in Kerek

A nationwide survey of regional handicrafts conducted in the 1970s brought the textiles of Kerek to the attention of the Tuban office of Indonesia's Department of Small Industries. In 1976 male officials, many of whom were neither locally born nor had any affinity for textiles, came to Kerek to conduct one-day workshops in the use of synthetic naphthol dyes. Small quantities of dyes and wooden dye troughs of the kind used in the batik industry were distributed in all the hamlet clusters in order to put the new technology into the hands of all women in the community, so that they could each earn additional income. The dyeing of cloth in Kerek, however, had always been a female occupation handed down within a small number of families residing in the central hamlets (by the 1970s only a single family remained). Halfhearted efforts made by the wife of the village chief to organize synthetic dyeing at her home collapsed after a few years, and much of the dyeing soon reverted to the premises of the hereditary dyers.

The use of naphthol dye for red was readily accepted in the 1970s because natural morinda, which had always been a purchased commodity, had disappeared from the markets in East Java early in the twentieth century, and only poor quality synthetic dyes had been available in the interim. Today the morinda dyeing process is no longer completely remembered in Kerek. For blue, on the other hand, the chemical dyes have never completely supplanted natural indigo, which is still valued in Kerek for the best-quality cloths for use within the area.

Made for sale, this shoulder cloth features a pattern and color combination that were newly created in the 1980s.

CAT. NO. 57
Woman's shoulder cloth (*sayut*)

Kerek, East Java, Indonesia, early 1980s. Batik on handspun/handwoven cotton cloth. Width 58 cm. X2002.37.87; GIFT OF E. M. BAKWIN. (NOT IN EXHIBITION)

Kerek cloth had always been made almost exclusively for local use, but in the 1980s a few locally born officials increased their efforts to bring outside attention to the unique batiks of the area. As a result, Kerek saw a rapid expansion in the production of cloth intended specifically for sale to outsiders. Certain features of the new batiks, such as the intermixing of local patterns and experimentations with new color combinations, made them unacceptable for use within Kerek.

Based on the growing popularity of Kerek batik, merchants from outside the community began to organize the production of so-called "Batik Tuban" in other parts of Java. Much of this cloth eventually made its way to buyers outside Indonesia who were in most cases unable to differentiate it from authentic Kerek batik. Eventually, it became possible to buy "Kerek-style" batik made on silk cloth (a fabric that was never used for locally produced batik in Kerek) in fashionable Jakarta department stores.

Today groups of young women in Kerek have established cooperative dye and batik undertakings (*sanggar*) in several of the hamlet clusters. They work primarily to fill outside orders. Women from the outlying hamlets who still make cloth for private use prefer to take it to a commercial dye shop that has been established conveniently close to the central market of Kerek. The difficulty of buying small quantities of synthetic dye powders, which entails a four-hour bus trip back and forth to Surabaya, has resulted in the persistence of dyeing as a professional or communal activity in Kerek.

The pattern of this shoulder cloth is a roughly waxed pastiche of motifs in the styles of various hamlets. The bright pink dyeing was done at a commercial dyeworks in Tuban town.

CAT. NO. 58
Woman's shoulder cloth (*sayut*)

Kerek and Tuban, East Java, Indonesia, 1980s–1990s. Batik on handspun/handwoven cotton cloth. Width 56 cm. X2002.37.99; GIFT OF E. M. BAKWIN. (NOT IN EXHIBITION)

The bright red color and tiny bud motifs on this skirt cloth are typical of Karanglo in the eastern hamlets, and the color combination is appropriate for a young married woman or for her baby's rituals. This, however, is a quickly made, recent cloth. The triangular bamboo shoot (*pucuk rebung*) motifs in the end borders are too short for an heirloom cloth, and the dots (*coblosan*) are not made individually but appear in straight running lines, indicating that a sewing machine was used to pierce the wax.

CAT. NO. 59
Woman's skirt cloth (*jarit*)

Karanglo (eastern hamlets), Kerek, East Java, Indonesia, 1980s–1990s. Batik on handspun/handwoven cotton cloth. Length 278 cm. X2002.37.86; GIFT OF E. M. BAKWIN. (NOT IN EXHIBITION)

This *sarung amba* bears a traditional pattern called *panji lori* in the *putihan* color combination, but the design has been simplified. It lacks the rectangular *bogeman* section in the central border, which has been reduced to the bamboo shoot (*pucuk rebung*) motifs alone.

CAT. NO. 60
Man's tubular skirt cloth (*sarung amba*)

Kerek, East Java, Indonesia, 1980s–1990s. Batik on handspun/hand-woven cotton cloth. Length 114 cm. X2002.37.79; GIFT OF E. M. BAKWIN. (NOT IN EXHIBITION)

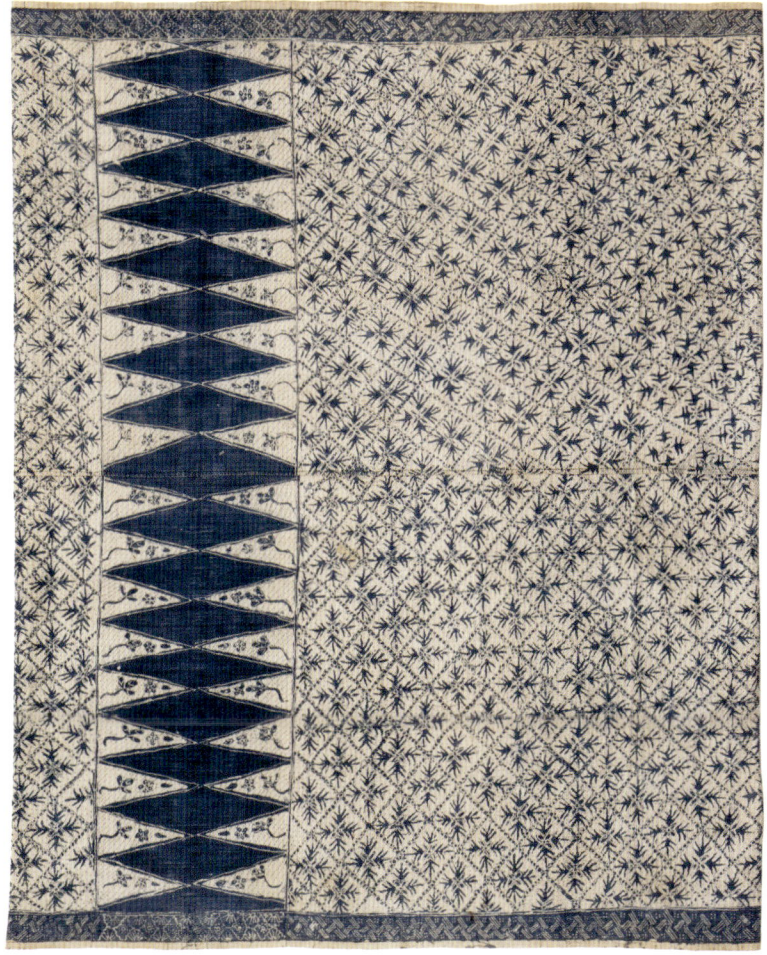

Batik in the Tuban Region

Although Kerek is the only place where a full range of cloth types was still made in the late twentieth century, cloth was once produced in many other villages in the Tuban region. During the Japanese occupation (1942–1945), commercial fabric disappeared from the market, leading to a revival of cotton cultivation and weaving. In addition to being used within the family, precious cloths also came to serve as welcome barter for other necessities. These practices continued in most places only into the mid-1960s, although in a few villages a trickle of cloth was still being produced as recently as the 1990s. The following localized traditions are of note:

Bongkol (or Brongkol), a hamlet in the village of Sumurgung located on the western outskirts of Tuban town, formerly produced batik on handwoven cloth. As in Kerek, there was a full range of color combinations, but the Bongkol names for these differed as did the specific local patterns (cat. nos. 61, 62, 64).

Bejagung, a village to the southeast of Tuban town, is the site of two sacred graves associated with the early history of Islam in the area. The wives of the hereditary guardians of the graves used to make blue-black batiks on handwoven cloth (cat. no. 63). The abstract patterns with small geometric motifs revealed the influence of the Chinese settlers who introduced the new faith in the coastal area in the early fifteenth century. A small amount of production for private use continued as recently as 1989. The base cloths were brought in from Kerek, while all the cloths were sent for dyeing to Kutorejo, a section of Tuban town where the ruler of Tuban once had his palace (*kraton*). By the late 1990s production had ceased.

Prunggahan, located southwest of Tuban town, is the site of the ruins of an old palace of the first ruler of Tuban. The making of batik on handwoven cloth for local use ceased there in the 1970s. Commercial batiks (*kain tukon*) made on industrially woven cloth continue to be produced because they are required as bridal gifts throughout the region. Although the color combinations resemble those of Central Javanese courtly batik, the large floral overlays and abstracted background patterns are specific to the eastern part of the North Coast. In Kerek *kain tukon* are used especially by the women of the southern hamlet in combination with a red *sayut* (see cat. no. 27) and by the wives of landless laborers and men who follow non-farming professions.

Gesikharja and Palang are two fishing villages on the coast east of Tuban town, where women used to earn income by making batik on industrially produced cotton cloth while the men were at sea. *Soga*, a reddish-brown dye, and indigo are responsible for the color combinations. The patterns feature prominent flowers and birds overlayed on a *gringsing* background (see cat. no. 47). These cloths are available in the markets of Tuban and sometimes in Kerek, used by the wives of non-farming professionals. The quality was good in the 1970s and 1980s, especially in years when subsidies were given by the Department of Small Industries. Production was still active as recently as the 1990s, but the quality diminished after the economic crash of 1997 when the imported dyes became too expensive.

Semanding and Karang are two villages located to the south of Tuban town. They still produce special batik headcloths that form part of the official dress of village chiefs (see fig. 5).

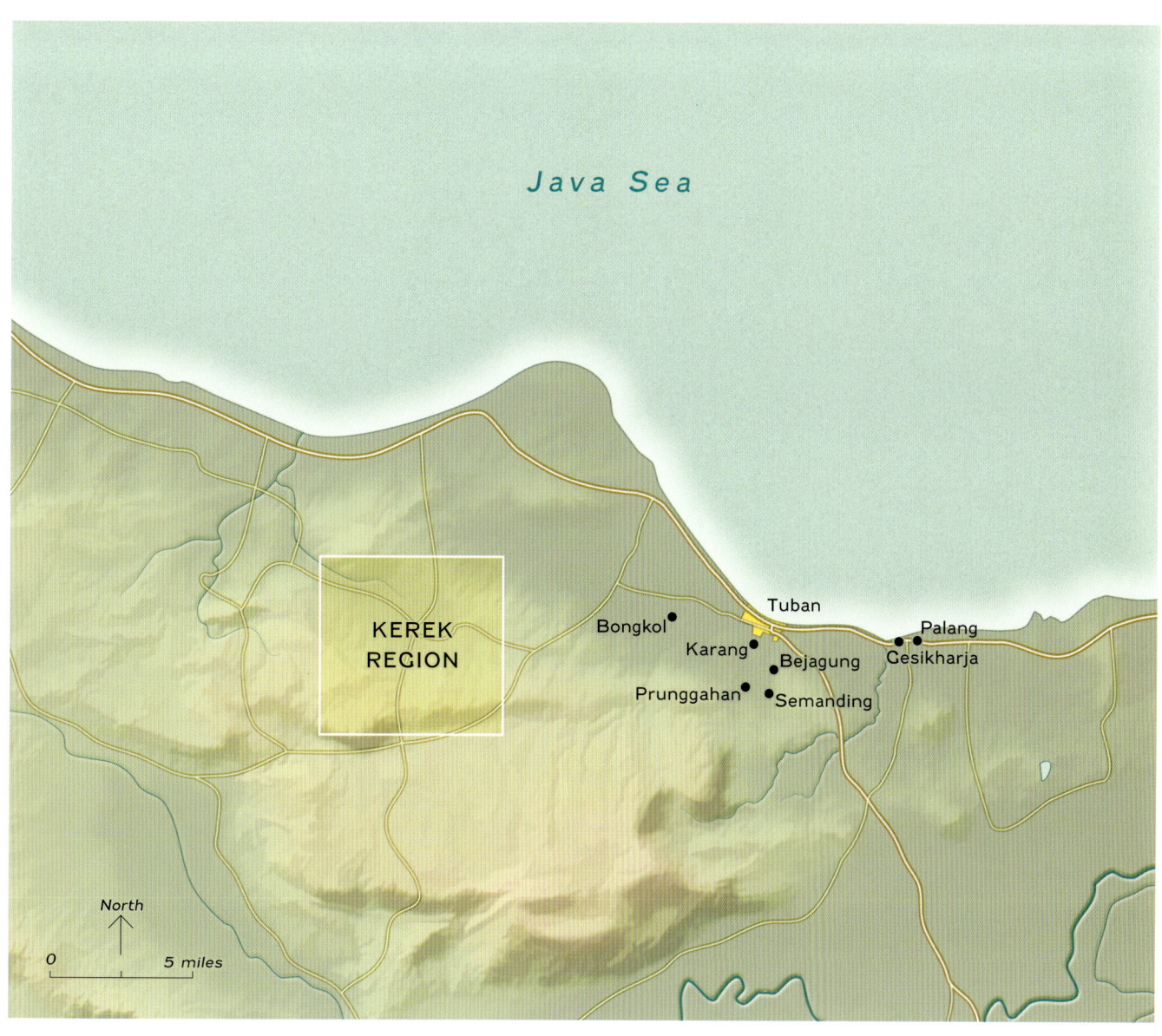

FIGURE 25
Villages in the Tuban region also once produced batik on handwoven cloth, but after the mid-1960s, this practice drastically declined.

This child's *sarung* was made by the Bongkol-born wife in a family of landowners in Luwuk, one of Kerek's northern hamlets. Marriage partners from Bongkol were sought after among the elite of Kerek, and the cloth was a circumcision gift for the son of the husband's younger brother, who was the village secretary (*carik*). The patterns represent a combination of the Bongkol style with elements drawn from commercial Tuban batik. The borders show European influences. This Bongkol color combination is referred to as *lodrok* or *lothek* (muddy), featuring tan motifs (from *soga*) rather than red on a crackled (muddy) plain ground.

CAT. NO. 61
Child's tubular skirt (*sarung anak*)

Bongkol, East Java, Indonesia, 1960s. Batik on handspun/handwoven cotton. Color combination: *lodrok* or *lothek*. Length 65 cm. X2008.10.27; PURCHASED BY FOWLER MUSEUM TEXTILE COUNCIL. (NOT IN EXHIBITION)

The robust but finely waxed floral and bird patterns on this Bongkol heirloom cloth are dyed bright red with morinda or blue-black with indigo. The *coblosan*, or dots, frequently appearing on Kerek cloths, are not part of the Bongkol tradition. The bird motifs include those known as *manuk huk*, which are also found on Kerek batik and on Chinese-Indonesian silk *lok can* shoulder cloths, and *manuk Burak*, the miraculous half-bird half-human mount of Muhammad. Young sprouts fill the background (*latar ungkeran*). The relatively long fringes are intricately knotted at their bases.

CAT. NO. 62
Woman's carrying cloth (*gendong*)

Bongkol, East Java, Indonesia, early twentieth century. Batik on handspun/handwoven cotton cloth. Color combination: *ungon*. Pattern name: *macanan* (like a tiger). Width 59 cm. X2009.10.1; PURCHASED BY FOWLER MUSEUM TEXTILE COUNCIL. (NOT IN EXHIBITION)

The color combination of this cloth, with white markings on a deep blue-black indigo ground without overdyes, is specific to Bejagung. The pattern, *cuken* (like a quilted mattress), is clearly related to the Chinese *banji* (ten thousand) motif. The technique and the appearance are quite distinct from the *cuken* made with the *batik lurik* technique in Kerek. The function of the cloth as expressed by the color combination and the pattern is to protect the caretakers of the ancestral graves.

CAT. NO. 63
Woman's shoulder cloth (*sayut*)

Bejagung, East Java, Indonesia, pre-1940. Batik on handspun/handwoven cotton cloth. Pattern name: *cuken* (like a quilted mattress). Width 52 cm. X2009.10.2; PURCHASED BY FOWLER MUSEUM TEXTILE COUNCIL. (NOT IN EXHIBITION)

The format of this cloth is similar to the *buntungan* from Kerek. It is worn by a post-menopausal woman and will be used as her shroud. The abstracted pattern *kenanga uleran* (ylang-ylang flowers eaten by caterpillars) is specific to Bongkol, while the color combination is *bironan* ("bluish," equivalent to *biron* in Kerek). According to local beliefs, this type of cloth should include the motif *kalajengkingan* (resembling a scorpion), which would increase its protective power.

CAT. NO. 64
Shroud

Bongkol, late nineteenth to early twentieth century. Batik on handspun/handwoven cotton cloth. Color combination: *bironan*. Pattern: *kenanga uleran*. Length 275 cm. X2008.26.17; GIFT OF MARY JANE LELAND. (NOT IN EXHIBITION)

DETAIL OF CAT. NO. 64

BATIK IN THE TUBAN REGION

GLOSSARY OF FREQUENTLY USED TERMS

bajra · textile motif consisting of ceremonial clubs that point in the four cardinal directions to ward off evil. The term comes from the Sanskrit *vajra*, meaning "thunderbolt."

baju cina · informal loose-fitting shirt worn by men with a wide, gusseted style of trousers (*sruwal*) for work on the land.

bakal kelambi · "basic material," fabric for a man's or woman's jacket.

bakal kutang · fabric for a woman's camisole.

bakalan · the "raw/original ones," the descendants of Kerek's first settled farmers, recognized as the original owners of the cultivated lands.

bang tegerang · a red and yellow color combination, appropriate especially for brides.

bangbangan · "reddened," a bright red and white cloth typical of the eastern hamlets and also well suited for brides.

bangrod · a contraction of *diabang* (reddened) and *dilorod* ("boiled," i.e., stripped of wax by boiling). A red and white color combination for batik.

banji · the Chinese "ten thousand" motif, a protective background motif in Kerek batik.

batik · wax-resist dyed process; also textiles made with this process.

batik lurik · batik produced on a *lurik* ground cloth. The checked pattern of the *lurik* provides a grid on which to make simple dotted batik patterns.

becek · dye derived from iron-rich *sawah* (wet rice field) mud, which produces a saturated black.

benang bola kuning · market-bought mercerized cotton yarn in the shape of a ball, yellow in color, used for supplementary weft.

biron · "bluish," a medium-dark blue color combination in Kerek batik.

bogeman · "place for valuables," sections of the field where special varieties of rice with ritual significance and protective properties are planted; also a design motif, which together with *pucuk rebung* (bamboo shoots) forms the border (*tumpal*) at each end of a *jarit* skirt cloth.

buntungan · "chopped off" or "lying fallow," a design format where the *tumpal* sections are missing. The pattern is carried over the entire surface of the cloth, enclosed only by a small white border. Worn by post-menopausal women and also used as wedding canopies and funeral shrouds.

camat · Indonesian civil service official in charge of a district (*kecamatan*).

canting · tool used to apply molten wax to cloth as part of the batik process.

celana gringsing · bridegroom's batik pants, blue-black with white patterns.

celana kagok · "informal trousers," tailored, knee-length pants in a loose Javanese style, formerly the traditional lower body garment for men.

coblosan · "pinpricked," small colored dots in the background of Kerek batik cloth.

gadung · "green," bright blue shade of indigo on batik and ikat cloth in Kerek.

galengan · small banks, as in a dry cultivated field; patterns running along the selvages of a *tapeh* skirt cloth.

gendongan · from *gendong* (to carry a child on the hip); a cloth used as a sling to carry a child in this manner. Only applied to a store-bought commercial batik.

glontor · drainage ditch; also an additional border at the end of the central design field (*pelemahan*) on a *jarit* skirt cloth.

gringsing · "against illness" (Old Javanese), simple batik patterns in white on a blue-black ground; color combination with protective properties.

irengan · "blackened," the darkest of Kerek's color combinations for cloth, ranging from dark blue to black.

jantra · spinning wheel.

jarit · a long rectangular batik for use as a woman's skirt cloth, in which the center field is *utuh* (whole) and the *tumpal* section *pecah* (broken in two). Metaphorically the design represents a wet rice field (*sawah*).

jarit buntungan · a *jarit* without *tumpal*, or border sections, which is intended for post-menopausal women.

jarit sisihan · a woman's batik skirt cloth with two different patterns in the central design field and also sometimes in the *tumpal* sections, one on the left and one on the right.

kain makau · industrially produced commercial cotton cloth imported to Java from the southern Chinese port of Macau until the early twentieth century for use as base cloth for batik.

kain tukon · "store-bought cloth," refers to commercial batik skirts worn by women who are not considered full members of the community, such as women from the southern hamlets, the categorical "to-be marrieds," and the wives of the large group of landless commoners. Today, better-quality *kain tukon* are used for everyday wear by all women.

Kalang · original forest inhabitants of the Kerek area.

kapas lawa · "fruit bat's cotton," natural brown cotton regarded as sacred.

kapas puteh mentah "raw white cotton," bolls of uncleaned cotton.

kayu tingi · tannin-rich bark of a mangrove (*Bruguiera* sp.) producing a red-brown dye.

kebaya · woman's upper garment, blouse, see *kelambi*.

kebayan · spokesman who mediates between the village chief and the populace.

kecamatan · the district administered by a *camat*.

kelambi · Javanese blouse or jacket tailored usually from commercial fabric, modern development prompted in part by long-standing Islamic influence.

kelambi rasukan · man's formal wedding jacket.

kembenan · "like a *kemben*," wearing a local cloth wrapped high over the breasts.

kentongan · hollow wooden or bamboo signal block that hangs outside the chief's house and is used to alert the community to emergencies.

kepek · basket with handles plaited from lontar leaf strips.

klenteng · Chinese temple.

kotongan · "empty body," checked *lurik* base cloth for making *batik lurik*.

kraton · palace compound.

krawangan · "open work," long elaborately knotted fringes.

kuli tani · landless laborers who work the fields belonging to others.

kutang · traditional form of camisole.

lalat menclat · "flies hovering close," stippled batik markings on fringe, a thinly veiled sexual metaphor for suitors hovering nearby.

laseman · "in the style of Lasem," pattern name that refers to a style associated with Lasem, the nearby center that is considered the place of origin for North Coast batik.

lawai · handspun cotton yarn.

lawon lawa · handwoven fabric of handspun natural brown cotton.

lelangit · "firmament-like," a wedding canopy. Also *langit-langit*.

lok can · Chinese-Indonesian silk shoulder cloth.

lurik · plain weave cotton cloth patterned with only stripes or checks.

lurik kembangan · "flowered *lurik*," cloth with small floral motifs, created with supplementary-weft or warp-float weaves.

lurik talenan · "tied-off *lurik*," cloth patterned using the ikat resist-dye process.

mengkudu · red dye from the root bark of trees of the genus *Morinda*.

nila · natural indigo dye.

patih · traditional assistant to the ruler, administrator of a region, *bupati* in the current Indonesian civil service.

pelemahan · "landed property," a cultivated field; also the name of the central design field of a *tapeh* or *jarit* skirt cloth.

pici · black velvet caps worn by men and now considered part of national dress.

pinggir · a double bund or dike surrounding a *pelemahan*, or cultivated field, in wet rice agriculture; metaphorically a border design surrounding the central design field of a *jarit* skirt cloth.

pinjungan · style of wrapping a skirt cloth high on the body, covering the breasts.

pipitan · "close together," red and blue color combination in Kerek batik; likened to the intimate relationships among husband, wife, and children.

pucuk rebung · "bamboo shoots"; also the triangular design motifs that in combination with the *bogeman* motif form the border (*tumpal*) at each end of a *jarit* skirt cloth.

pusaka · heirloom property.

putihan · "whitened" or "purified," white and blue color combination in Kerek batik.

salinan · "change of clothing," ritual conclusion of a Javanese wedding.

sarung · "sheath," woman's tubular skirt cloth.

sarung amba · "broad sheath," two-panel tubular skirt cloth for men, usually slung across the chest but also worn over the pants for formal occasions.

sarung anak · child's tubular skirt.

sarung talenan · ikat tube skirt.

sasrahan · "loan" of valuables—which includes a hoard of textiles—transferred by the kin of an elite groom to the bride one week before the wedding to entice her (*nrayuk*) to move in with her in-laws.

sawah · bunded fields that fill with rainwater, for growing wet rice.

sayut · "to bind together," long, narrow shoulder cloth for women, usually with fringe.

simpenan · "stored-away goods," heirlooms.

sisihan · design format for a woman's skirt cloth in which the main design field is divided into two differently patterned halves.

soga · reddish brown color or the natural dye materials to produce this color. Every area uses its own recipes to produce a preferred local shade. In Central Java the dye consists of a mixture of various tree barks.

sogo tingi · the reddish brown dye used in Kerek, made from the bark of a mangrove species, *kayu tingi*; only used as an overdye on indigo to further darken blue-black cloth.

sruwal · wide, gusseted style of trousers derived from a type originating in Persia; worn by men for work on the land, combined with an informal loose-fitting shirt (*baju cina*).

s(e)tagen · meters-long sash, tightly bound around the waist by women.

tapeh · "wrapper," long rectangular skirt cloth for women with woven or ikat patterning, but not batik.

tapeh benang sutera · woman's skirt cloth with silk supplementary-weft yarn.

tapeh talenan · "bound-off *tapeh*," woman's skirt cloth with ikat patterning.

tegal · dry field used primarily for growing maize and tuberous crops, the daily staples.

tegerang · the root of *Cudrania javanensis*, a yellow dye.

tengahan · "the central part," an open central lozenge on a cloth, a reference to the fertility of a bride.

tumpal · "border of a different color or pattern" (Old Javanese) at the two ends of a skirt cloth.

ungon · "purplish," overdye of light shades of red and blue. A relatively uncommon color combination in Kerek batik.

usik lawa · handwoven cotton fabric with the weft consisting of a two-ply yarn made with one strand of white cotton and one strand of natural brown cotton.

ABOUT THE AUTHOR

In 1954 Rens Heringa married an Indonesian medical student, whom she had met in Amsterdam, and in 1959 the couple settled in Surabaya. Heringa spent much of her adult life in Indonesia, raising five children, becoming fluent in Javanese, and studying Indonesian textile traditions. In 1985 she returned to The Netherlands to pursue formal studies in anthropology with an emphasis on textiles. Her many publications based on her continued research in rural East Java have provided a valuable counterpoint to the court-centric focus of most Javanese cultural studies. She is also a leading authority on the subject of batik. Heringa's bibliography follows:

1985   "Kain Tuban." In *Indigo: Leven in een kleur*, edited by Loan Oei, 115–20. Weesp: Fibula-van Dishoeck.

1988a   "Textiel en wereldbeeld in Tuban." In *Indonesia apa kabar? Oude traditres, nieuwe tijden*, edited by Reimar Schefold et al., 55–61. Meppel: Edu'Actief.

1988b   "Textiles and World View in Tuban." In *Indonesia in Focus: Ancient Traditions, Modern Times*, edited by Reimar Schefold et al., 55–61. Meppel: Edu'Actief.

1989   "Dye Process and Life Sequence: The Coloring of Textiles in an East-Javanese Village." In *To Speak with Cloth: Studies in Indonesian Textiles*, edited by Mattiebelle Gittinger, 107–30. Los Angeles: Museum of Cultural History.

1991a   "Textiles and the Social Fabric in Tuban." In *Indonesian Textiles: Symposium 1985*, edited by G. Völger and K. von Welck, 44–53. Ethnologica 14. Cologne: Rautenstrach Joest Museum.

1991b   "Kapas Lawa: Brown Cotton on Java." In *Indonesian Textiles: Symposium 1985*, edited by G. Völger and K. von Welck, 54–58. Ethnologica 14. Cologne: Rautenstrach Joest Museum.

1993a   "Tilling the Cloth and Weaving the Land: Textiles, Land, and Regeneration in an East-Javanese Area." In *Weaving Patterns of Life: Indonesian Textile Symposium 1991*, edited by Marie-Louise Nabholz-Kartaschoff et al., 155–76. Basel: Museum of Ethnography.

1993b   "Zinnebeeld van vrouwelijkheid." In *Lieve lasten: Hoe kinderen gedragen worden*, edited by I. C. van Hout, 95–100. Exhibition catalog. Amsterdam: Tropenmuseum.

1994   *Spiegels van ruimte en tijd*. Exhibition catalog. The Hague: Museon.

1997a   "Dewi Sri in Village Garb: Fertility, Myth, and Ritual in Northeast Java." In *The Divine Female in Indonesia*, edited by Robert Wessing, 355–77. Asian Folklore Studies 56, no. 2. Nagoya: Nanzan Institute for Religion and Culture.

1997b   "Ritual Cloth as Emblem of Socio-Religious Values: Introduction to a Comparative Panel of Indonesian Textiles." In *Sacred and Ceremonial Textiles, Proceedings of the 1997 Textile Society of America Symposium*. Washington, D.C.: Textile Society of America.

1997c   "Heirloom and Male Ancestors: The *Kain Kembangan* of East Java," contribution to "Ritual Cloth as Emblem of Socio-Religious Values." In *Sacred and Ceremonial Textiles: Proceedings of the 1997 Textile Society of America Symposium*. Washington, D.C.: Textile Society of America.

2000   "Function and Meaning of *Batik-Lurik*: A Reconstruction." In *Building on Batik: The Globalization of a Craft Community*, edited by Michael Hitchcock and Wiendu Nuryanti. University of North London, Voices in Development Management. Alderton: Ashgate.

2003   "Mbok Sri Dethroned: Changing Rice Rituals in Rural East Java." *The Art of Rice: Spirit and Sustenance in Asia*, edited by Roy W. Hamilton, 469–87. Los Angeles: UCLA Fowler Museum of Cultural History.

2007   "Reconstructing the Whole: Seven Months' Pregnancy Rituals in Kerek, East Java." In *Kinship and Food in Southeast Asia*, edited by Fiona Kerlogue and Monica Janowski. NIAS Studies in Southeast Asian Topics 38. Copenhagen: NIAS.

FOWLER MUSEUM AT UCLA

Marla C. Berns, *Shirley and Ralph Shapiro Director*
David Blair, *Associate Director*

Stacey Ravel Abarbanel, *Director of Marketing and Communications*
Patricia Rieff Anawalt, *Director, Center for the Study of Regional Dress*
Gassia Armenian, *Curatorial and Research Associate*
Manuel Baltodano, *Operations Supervisor/Technical Coodinator*
Sam Bartels, *Technical Support Consultant*
Danny Brauer, *Director of Publications*
Susan Chin, *Associate Registrar*
Sebastian M. Clough, *Director of Exhibitions*
Don Cole, *Museum Photographer*
Pablo Dominguez, *Financial Services Coordinator*
Bridget DuLong, *Events Manager*
Nicole A. Dunn, *Director of Development (through March 2010)*
Betsy Escandor, *Executive Assistant*
Luis Figueroa, *Weekend Operations Supervisor*
Gina Hall, *Manager of School and Teachers' Services*
Roy W. Hamilton, *Senior Curator of Asian and Pacific Collections*
Jo Q. Hill, *Director of Conservation*
Sue Kallick, *Assistant Store Manager*
Lynne Kostman, *Managing Editor*
Stella Krieger, *Store Manager*
Lori LaVelle, *Membership Coordinator*
Patricia Measures, *Assistant Conservator/Assistant Collections Manager*
Ruth Parsells, *Assistant Store Manager*
Patrick A. Polk, *Curator of Caribbean and Latin American Popular Arts*
Bonnie Poon, *Manager of Public Programs*
Betsy D. Quick, *Director of Education*
Rachel Raynor, *Collections Manager*
Roberto Salazar, *Human Resources Coordinator*
Mike Sessa, *Exhibitions Production Supervisor*
Barbara Belle Sloan, *Associate Director, Center for the Study of Regional Dress*
Agnes Stauber, *Digital Media Analyst*
Wendy Teeter, *Curator of Archaeology*
Emry Thomas, *Facilities Supervisor*